Dr David Ve[...]**st in** cognitive behaviour therapy at the South London and Maudsley Trust and the Priory Hospital North London. He is an Honorary Senior Lecturer at the Institute of Psychiatry, King's College London. He is an accredited cognitive behaviour therapist and was President of the British Association of Behavioural and Cognitive Psychotherapies (BABCP) in 2006–2008. He sat on the National Institute for Health and Clinical Excellence (NICE) working group that provided guidelines for treating Obsessive Compulsive Disorder and Body Dysmorphic Disorder in the UK.

Rob Willson is a cognitive behaviour therapist in private practice. He is a tutor at Goldsmiths College, University of London, and studying for a PhD at the Institute of Psychiatry, King's College London. He holds an Honours degree in Psychology, an MSc in Rational Emotive Behaviour Therapy and a Postgraduate Diploma in Social and Behavioural Health Studies. He has been involved in treating individuals with Obsessive Compulsive Disorder for over fifteen years. David Veale and Rob Willson are the authors of *Overcoming Obsessive Compulsive Disorder*, *Overcoming Body Image Problems including Body Dysmorphic Disorder*, *Overcoming Health Anxiety* and *Manage Your*[...] all published by Constable & Robinson, and Rob is the author of *Cognitive Behavioural Therapy for Dummies*.

TAKING CONTROL OF OCD

Inspirational Stories of Hope and Recovery

Edited by
DR DAVID VEALE
and
ROB WILLSON

Constable & Robinson Ltd
3 The Lanchesters
162 Fulham Palace Road
London W6 9ER
www.constablerobinson.com

First published in the UK by Robinson,
an imprint of Constable & Robinson Ltd, 2011

Important Note
This book is not intended as a substitute for medical advice or treatment.
Any person with a condition requiring medical attention should consult
a qualified medical practitioner or suitable therapist.

ISBN: 978-1-849-01401-4

Typeset in TW Typesetting, Plymouth, Devon

Printed and bound in the EU

1 3 5 7 9 10 8 6 4 2

Table of contents

What is OCD?

This is a unique book of inspirational stories written by 'real' people who have sought to overcome their own obsessive compulsive disorder. We'd like to extend our thanks to all of the people who have contributed to this book. We recognize that it takes courage to expose those aspects of themselves that, at one time at least, seemed the most shameful and abhorrent. OCD is a problem shrouded by shame, ignorance and pessimism. It is not uncommon for a person with OCD to suffer for ten years before they receive a diagnosis.

We hope this book will help individuals with OCD recognize that they are not alone with their problem. One of the things that's so exiting about hearing the stories of how people overcame their OCD is that it provides an opportunity to learn how they integrated a set of 'general' treatment principles to their unique personalities. Our aim in this chapter is to briefly outline *what* obsessive compulsive disorder (OCD) is and *how* it is usually overcome. We hope this will provide a reference from which the reader can consider the courageous journeys described in this book. For a more detailed explanation of OCD and how it can be beaten, please consult our book, *Overcoming*

Obsessive Compulsive Disorder, also published by Constable & Robinson.

OCD

OCD is the fourth most common psychological problem after depression, alcohol and substance abuse, and social phobia. Researchers estimate that about two in every hundred of the population have OCD at some time in their life. At least one in every hundred of the adult population is significantly distressed and handicapped by their OCD, and about one in every two hundred children and adolescents. The frequency is much the same all over the world, although the common forms of OCD may differ according to the culture.

In essence, OCD is a problem of trying too hard to reduce the threat of harm. The content of an obsession is usually what a person tries hard not to think about, or a kind of harm they particularly want to prevent. This might be a threat of harm to the self or other people, in the present or the future. People with OCD often feel that they have a pivotal responsibility for preventing or causing harm. This is often based on a misinterpretation that a 'mental event', a product of their mind such as an intrusive thought, image, doubt or impulse, is a threat in some way. For example, he or she may view them-selves as bad for having such thoughts or are worried that the anxiety will make them lose control and go mad. If you are a person with OCD, you might try to rid yourselves of these mental events by carrying out a compulsion or avoiding triggers, but several conse-quences can occur:

- The more you check something the more responsible you'll feel.
- The more you check something the more doubts you'll have.
- The more you try to neutralize or suppress a thought or image the more intrusive it will become.
- The more you analyse a thought the more significant your mind will interpret that thought as being, and therefore it will be more likely to draw your attention to it.
- The more you try to reduce threats the more aware of them you will become.
- The more you try to reassure yourself or get reassurance from others, the more your doubts return.
- The more you wash, the more likely you are to feel dirty and to wash again.
- The more you avoid something the more your fear of it will increase.

As you can see, *the solution is the problem*. Sometimes it *feels* like your solutions 'work' briefly (for example, they reduce anxiety or make you feel more certain) but then it gets worse. Overcoming OCD therefore usually involves the person re-training their brain to take less excessive levels of responsibility, and to treat intrusive thoughts and urges as part of very normal events in their mind, that should be allowed to simply happen. It means not responding to them and allowing yourself to just experience the thoughts and feelings.

Anxiety

Another key element of OCD is anxiety. Feeling anxious will make you more likely to jump to the worst conclusion, and will make catastrophic thoughts and images seem much more plausible: you may really start to believe that terrible, life-altering things are going to happen. Therefore, thinking and acting in ways that would be consistent with not being afraid, and 'facing' your fears, are a large part of recovering.

Other obsessional problems

There are a some other 'obsessional' problems that share similarities to OCD, including; 'health anxiety', in which a person is excessively preoccupied and distressed about the idea that they have or may contract an illness (this is covered in detail in our book, *Overcoming Health Anxiety*, published by Constable & Robinson); 'body dysmorphic disorder' (BDD) in which a person is excessively preoccupied with the idea that they are ugly (this is covered in detail in our book, *Overcoming Body Image Problems including Body Dysmorphic Disorder*). Compulsive hair-pulling (trichotillomania) and compulsive skin picking are also seen as related to OCD. All of these problems are similar in that refusing to participate in compulsions is the key to overcoming the problem.

Different kinds of OCD

Obsessive compulsive disorder can take many different forms. The various stories in this book represent most of the common ones. Below we introduce some of the different types. However, we could easily fill several volumes describing the many different variations of OCD so please don't be alarmed if what you read isn't 'exactly' you.

The most common kind of OCD is fear of contamination. This usually involves a fear of either causing harm or being harmed by germs, viruses, chemicals or other dangerous substances. Other than harm, some people with contamination obsessions are trying to avoid disgust. This is usually from sources such as bodily fluids and faeces. Researchers have also learned that some people with mental contamination do not need to have any physical contact to feel contaminated. They may have felt betrayed or violated in the past or may now fear having their personality 'contaminated' through association or contact with people they regard as undesirable. The most common 'safety' strategies related to contamination fears are avoidance of something or excessive washing. Washing might be of hands or body parts, or might include washing clothes, surfaces or items such as door handles.

Another common kind of obsession is the fear of being responsible for other kinds of harm such as the home being burgled or causing fire as a consequence of not being careful enough. The main strategies that people tend to use that maintain these fears are checking and giving up responsibility to someone else. An example of this kind of OCD is a fear of accidentally running someone over, leading the person to repeatedly retrace his or her journey or excessive checking in the rear-view mirror. An important understanding from research is that the more a person checks to make sure that they have not caused harm or failed to prevent harm, the more responsible and uncertain they feel. This is why stopping checking is so often a key part of recovering from OCD.

Around 7 per cent of obsessions focus upon the body or physical symptoms. This may have some overlap with health anxiety, in which a person fears that they may have an illness or are afraid that they may contract an illness. The more common concerns are cancer and AIDS/HIV, but it can be about any kind of physical or mental illness.

Another form of OCD is excessive concern with exactness, order or symmetry, such as excessively tidying and straightening up areas of the home or office. This might include excessively well-ordered bookcases, wardrobes, drawers, desks, kitchen cupboards and so on. This can make everyday activities very time-consuming, and can sometimes lead individuals with OCD to ban other people from areas of their home.

Religious obsessions, including fear of having sacrilegious or blasphemous thoughts, affect approximately 6 per cent of people who suffer from OCD. The responses that tend to maintain these obsessions include avoidance of religious people or places of worship, and repeating prayers until they are 'just right'. People with this kind of OCD may also try to replace their intrusive thoughts with 'correct' thoughts or images, or say phrases in their mind such as 'forgive me', 'no, no' or 'I don't mean it', or they may repeat the unwanted phrase in their mind to try and cancel out the original thought. They may avoid certain activities, objects or people so that they are not tainted with unwanted thoughts.

Inappropriate or unpleasant sexual thoughts or images are another common form of OCD. These thoughts are often surrounded by great shame and guilt. This can be a particular problem for individuals with OCD as it frequently prevents people from seeking help. This might take the form of thoughts or images of abusing children, babies or older adults, which the individual finds senseless and repulsive. The kinds of strategies that people employ that tend to reinforce sexual obsessions include trying to suppress or avoid thinking about certain topics; some people will tend to avoid sexually related activities altogether; and others will scan their bodies carefully to check for any 'inappropriate' bodily sensations. A particular problem in our modern times is the current moral panic and fear related to paedophiles. Of course, we recognize that child abuse is a very serious issue and occasionally people with OCD may have been abused when they were younger. However we also know that OCD is a problem that is not taken seriously enough. With this in mind we believe it is also very important that people with this kind of OCD reclaim the right to NOT worry about being a paedophile.

Hoarding obsessions can also occur in OCD. Here, a person collects items often regarded by others as excessive, useless, worn out, or of little or no practical value. The key here that the hoarding (as opposed to collecting for a hobby, for instance) is often linked to a fear of losing something important or a fear that they will, at some point in the future, regret throwing something away. The effect of hoarding, as with all OCD, can be devastating, often leaving the individual's home, or at least certain rooms, in chaos or squalor. Helping to overcome hoarding problems requires ruthless, rigorous separation of what is important, beautiful or valuable from that which is kept 'in case'.

Thoughts or images of violence and aggression – for example, stabbing a loved one – affect roughly one in twenty people who suffer from OCD. Individuals with these kinds of obsessions will frequently attempts to neutralize or 'remove' these thoughts. They may repeat certain activities, remove dangerous items such as knives from their home and carry out mental rituals such as saying special words in their mind. Such worries often occur in young mothers looking after a baby – the problem is not their risk of being alone with a child, but the suffering and handicap caused by the OCD.

Lastly people may sometimes experience intrusive nonsense words or music. This can be a particularly good illustration of what can happen if you try too hard to get rid of certain mental experiences. People sometimes worry that they are losing control of their minds and try desperately to push these experiences out of their mind, attempt to get to the bottom of 'why' they have them, or seek (or give themselves) frequent and excessive reassurance.

One of things we would like to stress very strongly is that the studies on intrusive thoughts in people with OCD and those in people without OCD have found no difference in the *content* of the thoughts, images, doubts or urges. It is only the interpretation of these events that differs between those who have OCD and those that do not that drives the increased frequency and intrusiveness of these mental events.

Overleaf is a list used in an important research study by S. Rachman and P. De Silva on OCD, in which ALL kinds of people, NOT just people with OCD, recognized experiencing the following kinds of NORMAL (if not always pleasant) thoughts:

1 *Impulse* to hurt or harm someone
2 *Impulse* to say something nasty and damning to someone
3 *Thought* of harm to, or death of, close friend or family member
4 *Thought* of acts of violence in sex
5 *Impulse* to crash car, when driving
6 *Thought*, 'Why should they do that? They shouldn't do that', in relation to people 'misbehaving'
7 *Impulse* to attack or strangle cats or kittens
8 *Thought*, 'I wish he/she were dead', with reference to persons close and dear, as well as to other people
9 *Thought* to harm partner with physical violence
10 *Impulse* to attack and violently punish someone, for example, to throw a child out of a bus
11 *Impulse* to engage in certain sexual practices that involve pain to the partner
12 *Thought*, 'Did I commit this crime?', when reading or viewing reports of crime
13 *Thought* that one might go berserk all of a sudden
14 *Thought* of wishing and imagining that someone close was hurt or harmed
15 *Impulse* to violently attack and kill a dog that one loved
16 *Thought*, 'These boys when they were young ...' – i.e. mechanically repeating a particular phrase
17 *Impulse* to attack or harm someone, especially own son, with bat, knife, or heavy object
18 *Thought* of unnatural sexual acts
19 *Thought* of hurting someone by doing something nasty, not physical violence, 'Would I or would I not do it?'

20 *Impulse* to be rude and say something nasty to people
21 *Thought* of putting obscene words in print
22 *Image* of mental picture of stabbing a passer-by
23 *Image* of mental picture of stripping in church

We hope that this helps you see that the weird and the wonderful are all part of normal human mental events! You simply can't choose what enters your head (nor should you as you'd lose all novel and creative thoughts that you'd never thought of before). You can only choose how you interpret and respond to what enters your head. Normalizing your thoughts, urges, doubts, impulses and images – that is, appreciating that they are just the sort of everyday thoughts that many people have – will be of enormous help in recovering from OCD. You can then start to learn how to give up your compulsions and face some of the fears that you have avoided.

Avoidance behaviour

One of the major ways in which OCD is maintained is by avoidance of the triggers for obsessions. Each time the person avoids a situation or activity the behaviour is reinforced because they have prevented themselves from experiencing anxiety and the harm that they think could have occurred. For example, if you avoid using public toilets because of the fear of contamination, you will have prevented yourself feeling anxious and your mind is likely to encourage you to avoid it again. Very often avoidance see-saws with compulsions – if you can't avoid something, you might create a ritual for dealing with it, or if rituals become very troublesome you might try even harder to avoid it.

Have I got OCD?

Only a trained health professional can diagnose you as suffering from OCD. The following is a screening questionnaire from the International Council on OCD.

1 Do you wash or clean a lot?
2 Do you check things a lot?
3 Is there any thought that keeps bothering you that you would like to get rid of but can't?
4 Do your activities take a long time to finish?
5 Are you concerned with orderliness or symmetry?

If you answered yes to one or more of these questions *and* it causes either significant distress *and/or* it interferes in your ability to work or study or your role as a homemaker, or in your social or family life or in relationships, then there is a significant chance that you have OCD. This test can be a bit over-sensitive to diagnosing OCD, so if you think you might have OCD, it is best to talk to a health professional and get appropriate help.

At what age does OCD begin?

Different individuals develop OCD at different ages. There is a group who develop OCD from about six onwards (more often boys). There is another group that starts to develop OCD during adolescence but the average age of onset is in the early twenties. The average age that men develop OCD is the late teens while women tend to develop it in the mid-twenties.

Who is vulnerable to developing OCD?

Like so many other kinds of psychological problems, there is no one 'type' of person who develops OCD. We've met people from all walks of life who have OCD, and it certainly has nothing to do with being 'weak' or 'crazy'. However, researchers have identified some psychological traits that may be associated with vulnerability to OCD. These include:

- Perfectionism
- Tending to be overly responsible
- Over-estimating the importance of thoughts
- Being intolerant of uncertainty
- Being generally anxious and a worrier

If you have OCD, and you recognize these tendencies, it will be well worth while trying to stop them in order to help you defeat your problem.

It is also possible that there are some genetic or biological factors that make people vulnerable to OCD, but generally psychological treatments have been by far the most successful. It's also possible that some early experiences, such as experiences of high levels of responsibility in childhood, may have a role to play. Ultimately everyone has their own unique blend of factors that led them to develop OCD: different journeys to the same address, if you like. However, the good news is that, whatever the route to developing OCD, most people respond well to very similar methods to help them get away from OCD and back to their lives.

Famous people with OCD

By way of illustrating that OCD can happen to all sorts of people, there are several famous or notable people who are thought or known to have suffered from OCD. It's becoming increasingly common to hear people mention OCD in the media, and sometimes popular personalities might refer to themselves as a 'bit OCD'. The following are some examples from history.

Howard Hughes (1905–76)

Hughes is one of the most famous individuals with OCD, and was played by Leonardo DiCaprio in a film about his life called *The Aviator*. Hughes' main obsession was a fear of contamination. He avoided sunlight, which he believed would encourage the growth of bacteria, and everything had to be handed to him covered in 'handles' of paper tissues so it did not come in contact with germs. When he died at the age of seventy-two in 1976, he was utterly isolated and in a state of total self-neglect.

Samuel Johnson (1709–84)

The author and creator of the first English dictionary, Samuel Johnson had both OCD and Tourette's syndrome and is reported to have carried out rituals when passing over the threshold of a door.

Charles Dickens (1812–70)

Charles Dickens may have had OCD. He had high levels of anxiety and was universally described as 'highly strung'. He had an obsession for ordering the furniture in any room in which he stayed or worked to try to achieve its exactly 'correct' position. Certain objects had to be touched three times for luck. Dickens also compulsively tidied up after others and was angered by sloppiness.

Hans Christian Andersen (1805–75)

Hans Christian Andersen was a famous Danish writer of fairy tales who it is thought had OCD and depression. He would become obsessed that something he had just eaten would poison him or would exaggerate some trivial event to the point that he thought it would lead to his death. Most nights, he repeatedly rose from his bed in order to check that he had extinguished the candle by his bed, though he had never failed to do so. Andersen would often worry that he had paid the wrong amount in a shop or that he had mixed up the envelopes of the letters he had sent.

What triggers OCD?

The factors that might trigger or 'switch on' OCD are relatively unknown, and it usually begins gradually. You may be one of the 50 per cent of OCD individuals for whom there were no specific triggers. However, individuals with OCD are more likely than individuals without OCD to have had one or more life-altering events in the six months prior to the onset of their OCD. Some individuals report a specific event such as having a child that led to OCD being triggered. For others, a trauma such as rape, an accident or other bad experiences such as bullying or conflict may 'switch on' or aggravate OCD.

Treatments for OCD

The main treatments for OCD are cognitive behaviour therapy (CBT), which includes exposure and response prevention (ERP). More severe symptoms usually require antidepressant medication. Medication may be used in combination with psychological therapy or alone. In general, you are less likely to relapse if you do CBT/ERP than medication alone. One of the things that can be a bit confusing about overcoming a problem that can feel as tough and complicated as OCD is that the treatment principles can seem relatively simple. And indeed in many ways they are: it's just that *simple* does not necessarily mean *easy*. That said, quite often the key to solving any problem, OCD included, is understanding the true nature of the problem (e.g. that the real problem is excessive worry about being dangerous rather than in fact being dangerous). Once you become clearer on the nature of the problem it's easier to pick the right solution. In the case of overcoming OCD it may be that you've been trying too hard to be safe, or to rid your mind of certain thoughts. In this sense recovery can be seen as both keeping things a bit simpler and taking it a bit easier!

CBT is available both on the NHS and privately in the UK, and private treatment is not a guarantee of better quality. The most important thing is to make sure that you get treatment from an appropriately trained therapist whom you feel understands your problem well, and has robust determination to help you beat it. The charity OCD Action has produced a leaflet which provides advice on how to access treatment for OCD on the NHS and privately which you can download from their website. They have also produced a checklist to help you work out whether or not the treatment you are receiving is CBT which is also available from their website. Their contact details are listed under 'Support Groups and Charities' at the back of this book.

Exposure and response prevention (ERP)

This occurs when a person with OCD repeatedly confronts the situations or activities that he or she has avoided without doing a compulsion (technically called 'response prevention' or sometimes 'ritual prevention) until the anxiety has subsided. This is the cornerstone of psychological treatment and the process of letting the anxiety reduce is known as 'habituation'. It also helps you to find out whether what you expect to happen does in fact happen and to learn new ways of behaving by acting against the way you feel.

Cognitive behaviour therapy (CBT)

Exposure may also be part of a formal 'behavioural experiment' where you are testing out some of your feared consequences (for example, the belief that when you are very anxious that it will go on forever if you don't carry out a ritual).

The cornerstone of CBT for OCD is to test out whether what you learn in an experiment fits best with two *competing* theories:

1 Theory A: you are at high risk of causing harm or failing to prevent harm. Your solution is to try hard to reduce this risk. Unfortunately your solution of compulsions and avoidance then becomes your problem and feeds your worries.
2 Theory B: you worry excessively about causing harm or failing to prevent harm. If the problem is of worry, then the solution is completely different to Theory A and involves acting against your bully to overcome your worries.

Breaking free from OCD

One of the most important things to consider about overcoming OCD is that overcoming OCD *in itself* is not the point. The *point* is to live in a way that you find rewarding, that is consistent with being the kind of person you want to be, and that is consistent with contributing to the kind of world you want to live in. This will almost certainly not involve endless hours of your life engaged in ruminating, analysing, checking and avoiding. Despite your intention, you, your loved ones or the world around you do not feel in any way protected or cared for by your OCD. Assuming you have OCD, if your current strategies were working it's unlikely that you would be still be having your fears.

Here are some key ways in which you can lessen your OCD and improve your life.

1 Imagine how you would like to be different, in terms of how you feel and behave. Picture yourself being this way in your mind's eye.

2 List all of your hopes, dreams and aspirations. Imagine how being utterly free from OCD would help you towards them.

3 Develop a mental image that represents your OCD when it is trying to force you to carry out a mental or behavioural ritual – a bully, a demon, a computer virus, Nazi propaganda on a radio or choose your own mental image.

4 Develop a mental image that represents defeating your OCD.

5 Find inspiration for overcoming adversity – choose a role model or metaphor that helps you to stick with progress and resist the urges to check, wash, seek reassurance, review or analyse in your mind.

6 Identify someone who you can share (and celebrate) your progress with. Help them to see that you need cheering on in your progress, NOT reassurance or debates over safety etc!

7 List all of the strategies that you employ in your mind and in your behaviour that are maintaining your OCD. View these like bad habits you are going to train yourself out of and do not respond to such urges by giving yourself reassurance or try to suppress such thoughts and urges.

8 Imagine that you have a twin, who is the same as you in every respect, but is free from OCD, and use them as your guide in changing your behaviour.

9 Test out treating your problem 'as if' it's a problem of worrying too much or being too cautious. The trick is to do this *even though you're not 100 per cent sure*. Remember that looking for certainty is very much the problem, not the solution.

10 Find a metaphor for treating intrusive thoughts as events just passing through your mind. Traffic passing in the street or leaves on a river are just a couple of examples. The trick is to allow your mind to take care of itself, without interfering with or responding to the intrusive thoughts. The flow of thoughts in your mind should be as much left to its own devices as the blood flowing through your veins.

11 Deliberately practice refocusing your attention on to the things you can see, hear, smell and feel in the 'real' outside world, here and now.

12 NORMALIZE your doubts, images, thoughts and impulses. This means fully accepting that your intrusive thoughts, images and doubts are normal and part of being human.

13 Embrace each time you have an intrusive doubt, image, thought or impulse as an opportunity to accept them willingly into your mind. Think of it as keeping your friends close and your enemies closer!

14 Practice assuming the best. OCD has a habit of knocking your rose-tinted spectacles off so get back to normal by assuming the best rather than the worst.

15 Listen to music that helps you to get into the frame of mind to drive your true values and aspirations straight through OCD and out the other side.

16 Focus on *getting* better, more than *feeling* better. Measure your progress in terms of your levels of distress and ability to function across the course of a couple of weeks.

17 'OCD loves a vacuum!' As you recover, fill the gaps in your life that your OCD might leave behind with hobbies, exercise, education, friendships, deepening relationships with loved ones or furthering your career. There's evidence that doing so will help you keep OCD out of your life.

Trying to overcome OCD is tough, but it's even tougher if you don't attempt to and the rewards are enormous. Hopefully your fellow travellers in the following chapters will help you to see that you are not alone and inspire you to keep going, or perhaps something they have written will help you to start making changes. These are 'real life' experiences, and you may find that there are both similarities and differences to your own experience. No matter what, don't give up. If you seek help from a healthcare professional, don't accept a poor level of understanding and pessimism. OCD *can* be overcome and you have the right to be free from excessive anxiety, guilt, obsessions and compulsions.

David Veale and Rob Willson

1

Life-changing events

The start of a nightmare

My life changed the moment I heard. It really was as simple as that.

Aged twenty-seven, I had recently moved in with my long-term girlfriend. I had a good job, and – after three years or so – I was doing reasonably well at it. I had a good set of friends, and life was – on the whole – going pretty well. Most people who knew me would think I had few cares in the world. And on the face of it, the future looked pretty good.

Then a colleague of mine committed suicide. I remember very vividly being told the news by my boss, and thinking immediately that something very major had changed in my life. Suicide might cause anyone to be upset, you might think. And I guess you'd be right, except that nobody else seemed to react in quite the same way as I did. I know that because I spent the weeks after his death anxiously monitoring other people to see if it was having the same effect on them as it seemed be having on me. In time, most people seemed to be able to get back on an even keel, and the smiles and laughter in the office gradually returned. Not for me though. I couldn't work out why: he

wasn't a good friend, or even an especially close colleague. But something about what he had done, and how
he had done it, had a profound effect on me.

In the weeks following his death, I just could not shift it
from my mind. I deliberately avoided his funeral, fearing
that it might make me feel worse. And it soon became
obvious to me that what I was experiencing was not
conventional mourning, but something altogether weir-
der. I felt desperately sorry for him and for his family, but
– alongside that – I began to become inundated with
thoughts about my own suicide. Five years on, I can talk
about it quite freely, but at the time it was horrendous: I
could barely see anything which didn't remind me of
killing myself. Every time I crossed the road, I pondered
what would happen if I stopped moving and was run over
by a bus. Using the Underground was even more of a
nightmare. I was plagued by thoughts of jumping in front
of the oncoming trains.

The volume and content of this type of thoughts caused
me to be extremely worried. They must mean something
about me, I thought. Perhaps my former colleague had
had them before he killed himself? Is this what happens
to people about to commit suicide, I kept wondering. I
spent a long time analysing precisely what the meaning
could be. But, while I was trying to figure it all out in my
mind, I thought the most sensible thing to do was not to
run the risk of a suicidal event actually happening. So I
effectively shut down: I stopped using the Underground,
and began adopting (often quite bizarre) tactics to limit
my exposure to what I thought were 'life-threatening'
situations. I barely told anyone about what was going on.
I didn't know where to start.

Gradually, the thoughts began to invade every part of my everyday life. Medicines in the cupboard, bleach at the supermarket, knives in the kitchen – you name it, my brain could conjure ways in which everyday items could kill me. Whatever I was doing, wherever I was, whoever I was with, try as I might, I just couldn't chase the thoughts out of my head.

What was really bothering me about all this was not actually the end of my own life. Don't get me wrong, though – that didn't exactly thrill me either. But I remember spending hours and days deliberating the effects that my own suicide might have on those who I loved. I would, in some detail, try and picture what my girl-friend would do, how my parents would react, what my sisters would do. I also remember trying to gauge how colleagues at work would deal with another suicide within such a short space of time. But throughout it all I was totally confused: I didn't want to kill myself, so why was I having so many thoughts about doing exactly that?

Living your life to a script like this does not make for comedy. The recurrent thoughts about my own death and, primarily, its effects on other people gradually drained all the colour from my life. I was obsessed by the thoughts, and apart from very short periods when I was completely engaged in something else, it felt as if I was thinking of nothing else. I didn't want to eat and had lost weight (but in that ill-looking way that makes people frown at you sympathetically, rather than in a training for the marathon way that wins admiring glances); I couldn't concentrate at work; and I had lost any interest in doing any of the things that I used to enjoy.

Unless you're a hermit, when this sort of thing happens

it is quite difficult for other people not to notice. And it had become increasingly obvious to everyone who knew me that something was wrong. By this stage, I had spoken to my girlfriend about it, but I couldn't seem to articulate the problem. Of course, it's all very clear now what was going on. But back then I had never really heard of anything like it. I thought I was unique (but not in a good way!).

At that time, if I thought anything about it at all, I probably thought OCD was all about triple-checking that you had locked your front door, and that your chest of drawers was tidy. I was pretty ignorant. And my knowledge of wider mental health issues wasn't much better either. So, in trying to explain what was going on to my girlfriend and – later on – to my parents, I couldn't seem to see any pattern or trend in what was happening to me. And I couldn't really describe it all in any way that made any sense to anyone else.

Getting professional help

Eventually, with encouragement from my girlfriend and my family, I went to speak to someone about the problem. First, I saw a GP. We went through the chronology of what had happened, and I touched on some of the difficulties I was having. I can't really remember what I said, but I don't recall being too expansive about the strange thoughts. I remember we concentrated more on my lack of appetite and sleeping patterns – the effects, in other words, more than the cause. He said I was probably depressed. By that stage I wasn't in a position to disagree.

On the doctor's recommendation, I went to see a counsellor. My girlfriend had found the name of one for me on the recommendation of a friend, and convinced me that it was a sensible thing to do. But I can remember being embarrassed about the whole thing. I was a twenty-seven-year-old man who liked drinking, playing football and – for want of a more accurate pigeonhole – bore the hallmarks of an aspirant alpha male. Going to see a counsellor didn't seem to be consistent with that. I certainly didn't know anyone else in my group of friends who had ever done it, or rather, I didn't know anyone who had ever told me about it!

So along I went to my first session with what turned out to be a very friendly counsellor in north London. The first few sessions went well, in the sense that we got on and I could tell her about what had been happening. But she could never quite figure out what really was going on with me. We went through my – mostly pretty happy – childhood, and my – again, pretty conventional and happy – family background and she kept drawing blanks. There didn't seem to be some great big burning issue in my past that was triggering the problem. Yes, I had been to boarding school. But no, I hadn't hated it. Yes, my parents had lived away from me when I was at school. But no, I had a good relationship with them, loved them and had never felt unloved in return. My relationships with the rest of my family were good, and we saw each other regularly. I loved my girlfriend; no, I wasn't having an affair with the secretary. I didn't really have any enemies (that I knew of, at least). We went through everything. Well, almost everything.

After about five sessions, I finally owned up to the fact that this was not the first time in my life that I'd had these strange, intrusive, recurring thoughts. And some of the things that I thought about, I explained, were actually a lot worse.

Opening up

I don't know how you're supposed to tell someone you don't know that you have thoughts about killing people you love. It's not something you can slip into a conversation about how late the daffodils bloomed this year. In fact, I had never told anyone about it before. Looking back, I am surprised I ever found the wherewithal to raise it with the counsellor at all. And I remember being surprised that she didn't immediately call the police as I told her how – at various stages in my life – I had struggled to cope with violent, shocking, beastly, wicked thoughts about murdering people I love. It didn't matter how many times I told her that I never actually wanted to do these things – I kept trying to stress that they appalled me and made me profoundly sad – when the words came out of my mouth, I felt like a truly evil creature.

Looking back, the counsellor deserves a medal. She listened intently, but never once showed any signs of being shocked. I remember that I cried a lot. I also remember that she was sympathetic (and seemingly not calling for outside help while I sat there wiping the tears away). After I had spat out my terrible secret to her, she told me that an assessment with a psychiatrist was probably what was needed. That terrified me. But in the interests of safeguarding those I loved most from the beast that clearly lived inside me, I remember thinking it was probably a sensible idea. In my mind, I was convinced that seeing a psychiatrist was the first step on an inevitable path to being put in some kind of secure institution. Scared as I was, I remember thinking it was probably the best place for me.

The diagnosis

Ten days or so later, after a referral from my GP, I went to see an NHS psychiatrist. I remember thinking that perhaps I ought to pack some extra clothes, in case the psychiatrist sent me straight off to the prison I had in my mind. I remember that I went with my girlfriend, my sister and her little dog. Going with people I knew calmed me down a little bit and the dog made things a bit more human. But it turns out that seeing a psychiatrist isn't quite what I had envisaged. Yes, the building I went to wasn't what you would call a home from home. But there were no padded cells (that I could see, anyway), and the lady I spoke to was about my age and not remotely scary. My counsellor had written a letter following our meeting, and the psychiatrist had read it before I arrived. After a thirty-minute chat and a few tears (from me, rather than the psychiatrist!) she told me I had OCD and secondary depression. She prescribed something called cognitive behaviour therapy (CBT) and a dose of antidepressants.

That half-hour meeting changed the course of my life. Not least because she hadn't dispatched me to the secure institution I had thought would be home for the rest of my time. Instead I got to go home afterwards ...

Following the diagnosis, I was so elated that it wasn't just me who had this problem, and that having it didn't necessarily guarantee that I would one day feature on *Crimewatch* (I had always hated that programme precisely because I thought I would one day be on it). The psychiatrist had told me I had several options: the NHS would provide CBT, but there was a long waiting list, she said. Or, I could get the same treatment privately. However, I could get going with the pills immediately. So I did.

I spent most of the next two weeks or so reading everything I could about OCD. So did my girlfriend and family. A wave of euphoria crept over me as I learned that what I had was a recognized condition and that there are things you can do to get better. Looking back, I think I confused the diagnosis with the cure. The reality is that it took me a lot of time to get my life back together. But at the time, things were definitely looking up.

The start of a comeback

I guess that from learning about the suicide of my colleague to being given a diagnosis took about three months. During that time I had seen and spoken to four professionals about the issue. But in those three months, I had become a shadow of the person I was. I was thin and withdrawn, and not much fun to be around generally. I was crying a lot of the time, and occasionally felt that life was not really worth living if it was going to be like this. So, in the wake of the diagnosis, I took some time off work and went to stay with my parents for a while. My bosses at work were brilliant – they had by this stage twigged that something wasn't quite right, and gave me a lot of encouragement as well as the time off.

Moving back in with my parents – and, in doing so, leaving my girlfriend behind – was awful, but she had a full-time job and I just didn't feel capable of dealing with long spells alone each day. I was slightly embarrassed about barging in on my parents' semi-retirement – what twenty-seven-year-old wants to be living at home with his mum and dad? It wasn't exactly part of my big plan for life. But they were fantastic: it was the first time we had lived together for ages, and they did all they could to welcome me home. Incidentally, when I look back on this period (and when I am in an objective frame of mind), I do think one of the positives of having been through all of this is the effect it has had on my relationship with my family. It is humbling to think how much love and support they have given me over the last five years.

After the diagnosis, I changed therapists and went to see a one who specializes specifically in CBT. Gradually, it became clear that nothing I could tell him about my thoughts scared him. And so I opened up about the true extent of them. I told him about all of the many and varied gremlins that I had which – to my mind – made me an evil person. He told me that nearly all of them were pretty textbook for someone with OCD. Besides what he told me himself, the therapist gave me a reading list of books to read on the subject, which my family and I duly devoured, trying to learn as much as possible, as quickly as possible.

At the same time as reading the books, over several sessions the therapist gradually managed to demonstrate to me that I had what he described as 'maladaptive' perceptions of the world and in particular my sense of responsibility in it. Basically, insofar as there was a cause for what was happening, it was a heightened sense of my own responsibility. As a result, among other things I had done was to fuse together the idea of a frightening thought with the belief that I might act on it. And in turn, he told me, because I didn't want to harm anyone else I had more thoughts of doing exactly that than the national average (which is already surprisingly high, based on studies he showed me). Essentially, he was trying to point out, everyone in the world gets weird thoughts.

The format was that I would see the therapist once a week and do 'homework' between the meetings. The homework mostly consisted of trying to overhaul the system I had put in place for coping with the dreaded thoughts. It seems what I had thought were really clever tactics for coping with them had apparently been pretty conventional, too (and had served to make the problem worse). Mostly, those tactics had been to avoid scenarios when the thoughts would typically occur. As I mentioned, I had all but stopped using public transport. I had also removed certain knives from kitchen drawers which triggered the thoughts, and moved medicines from the cupboards at home so I didn't have to see them every day. I tried to limit seeing or hearing about anything that might prompt thoughts about me harming others.

Overhauling all of this took some time. I had to do all sorts of different things to try to test whether the horrible thoughts and images I had were meaningful, and to try to get used to them: I stood repeatedly on railway bridges, willing the suicidal thoughts on; I used a chainsaw to cut up logs, trying to dream up horrendous massacre scenarios; I carried a penknife on walks with my family. There were lots of other exercises, too. All of them felt totally alien, and – in some cases – caused me massive amounts of anxiety. I genuinely thought that I was risking mine and other people's lives by doing these things, and occasionally thought that the therapist was mad for getting me to do them. But he calmly explained the principles of exposure and actively encouraged me to carry on. Fortified by his explanations, in the space of three months I put myself in all sorts of scenarios I would always have avoided in the past.

Challenging my strategy of avoidance proved pretty successful, and before long I was beginning to learn that there is not an automatic fusion between thoughts and actions. Effectively, I had begun to appreciate that you can think anything you like (or, more often than not, don't like) and not have to take steps to prevent those thoughts from becoming a reality. That was progress. Over the space of the next couple of months, I stopped living with my parents and moved back to my girlfriend, returning to work at the same time.

In preparation for all of this, I had found some support groups for OCD sufferers that I thought might be useful. In some ways, they were. It was interesting to meet other people who experienced similar problems and hear from them how they were dealing with them. Some seemed to have a good understanding of CBT; others had only recently started to try to get help. Some were on medication, others weren't. I didn't go to hundreds of meetings, but I went to a few. Some people swear by them; other people hate them. The only suggestion I can think of is to go and see for yourself.

When you're grappling with CBT but not quite there yet, it can be useful to have something else to focus on. Sport was quite helpful for me. There is something about the concentration levels and focus required to play most sports that is completely absorbing, and therefore refreshing. I found squash particularly useful for that. Football is pretty good, too. Cricket is all right when you are batting, but fielding for hours on end tends to mean a lot of time for your brain to wander. But in general terms, I have always found sport of any kind really to be an excellent relief from a cluttered brain, albeit that the relief is temporary. It's clearly not a solution on its own, but it can help.

A major hurdle

Although, on paper, I was living my life normally, I was not totally converted. I was still struggling to believe that the thoughts – at some level at least – did not mean something about me. I couldn't quite believe that they didn't somehow signify that I was fundamentally an evil person. I still was not convinced that it was safe to have them, and that I didn't need to chase them out of my head. And it was around this time that the thoughts began to take a different turn. To date, most of what I had worried about was based around my own death or about the death or injury of others. The thoughts now began to turn to my sexual orientation. In particular, I began to think that in addition to being a suicidal serial killer, perhaps I was also a paedophile. That is far from a winning combination, in anyone's book.

You might think that, having learned a little about the theory behind the thoughts, I could easily dismiss these new ones. But I couldn't. The content of what was now floating around my head felt so revolting that a new wave of shock and self-loathing overcame me. Of all of the themes of thoughts I have ever had (and there have since been others, too) the idea that I might be a paedophile has been the most difficult to come to terms with. I found myself avoiding all over again – this time any scenarios where there might be children, any newspaper reports of paedophiles (of which, it seems, there are hundreds published every day) and any other scenarios which might trigger the thoughts. My natural tendency was to fight the thoughts, disprove them, reason with them – anything to make them less frightening. Anything to make them go away. These new ones seemed to fall outside the boundaries of any of the techniques and theory I had learned. They were just too serious to risk taking any chances with, I thought.

Having taken several steps forward, I was now back to being profoundly miserable again. I felt incredibly depressed. Gradually, the secondary depression made its own bid for pole position, and I was in a mess again. I had stopped eating properly, I wasn't sleeping and I had no energy to do anything. Things kept getting worse as I battled day and night trying to evict the uninvited thoughts from my head. So much so, I had to take even more time off work, and again moved back in with my parents. Groundhog Day.

This period marked the low water mark of my OCD experience. I don't think I have ever been so unhappy, and there were times when it didn't seem worth carrying on. I would dread the moment, one or two seconds after waking up each morning, when the wave of new thoughts would come into my head. Each day seemed to go downhill from that moment on. The only thing I wanted to do was sleep. Sleep offered what I thought was the best chance of stopping the flow of the thoughts. The rest of the time, I was bad-tempered, miserable to be around and crying nearly all of the time. I just couldn't see any way ahead.

Given that this is a positive story, it doesn't make much sense to dwell too long here on how bad things were. Suffice to say, I didn't know it was possible to feel such aching loneliness and unhappiness. When I look back on how dismally wretched the situation had become, my memories still have the capacity to shock and upset me. But in time, and by that I mean about six months of seeing a therapist regularly, and of applying the same core techniques, I gradually began to escape the dark place my head had become.

The present

Three years later, I have been slowly able to come to terms with my OCD. There are even times when I can laugh at what's going through my mind. A few years ago, the same thoughts would have paralysed me with fear. The thoughts I have are mostly based around the same core themes: suicide, murder and being some kind of sexual deviant. None of which is the stuff of dreams, obviously, but it's not the end of the world either. I have gradually come to realize that the particular content of one thought or another doesn't really matter. The reality is that they are all unwanted; they are all part of the same problem; and the way to deal with all of them is the same.

I still see a different therapist – this one a specialist in OCD and based closer to home – but less often than before. And, when I knock on the door at the beginning of each session with him, I sometimes think how things have changed since I was diagnosed with OCD. When I went to my first session with him, he and I sat down and discussed what was important to me, what my goals in life were and what sort of a person I wanted to be. And there are tangible achievements I can point to over the last three years where I have successfully overcome my OCD to achieve these goals.

Easily the biggest achievement is that I successfully convinced my longstanding girlfriend to marry me. During the worst times I had struggled to like myself and the idea that somebody else might love me enough to spend the rest of their life with me, warts and all, was pretty staggering. Throughout everything we have been through with the OCD she has supported me totally, not reading too much into the thoughts that were in my head. She has told me that she sees them as a mental misfire somewhere in my brain. At various stages, she has had more confidence in me than I have often had in myself. I hope that I would have shown the same patience and love if she were in the same position. The day we got married really felt like the conclusion of all of the pain of the last few years. I had worried for ages that it might never happen or that if it did, I would be so desperate for the thoughts not to overcome me at some key moment that I wouldn't be able to enjoy it. I barely noticed them.

There are other achievements, too. We have bought a house together, for example. Previously, I had thought this was a step too far: what if I did commit suicide, and she was left to make the repayments by herself? I have also been promoted several times at work, and have recently been offered the chance to live and work abroad. I feel I have repaid the faith shown in me by my company and colleagues. And, while these things may not seem like much, at one stage or another in the past they all seemed completely out of reach when I was in the depths of despair with my OCD. More to the point, to me they seem like illustrations of someone who is doing more than just existing. They seem like signs of someone who is pursuing life.

But it's also in the small things where I can see a major difference between who I was and who I am now. I don't dread the mornings anymore; I can spend time by myself, alone with my thoughts; I can read newspapers without fear that an unexpected article will throw me into a panic; I can hear the sound of birds in spring and feel a surge of happiness inside me that confirms that life really is worth living. Reading that last line again, I can hear that it sounds like a cliché. But when I was in the midst of despair, I wouldn't have known (or cared) whether the birds were singing or not. I was completely focused on what was going on in my head, to the exclusion of all else. I didn't see or hear what was going on around me at all. In the process, I ignored some of the really amazing things that can happen day-to-day, and which have the capacity to brighten your life.

Other upsides

Don't get me wrong, life is not perfect. I never did become a professional footballer. In fact, I have remained resolutely terrible at football throughout. But I can't realistically blame that on the OCD. And – regardless of the OCD – I have the same good and bad days that everyone else enjoys and suffers, at work and at home.

The disorder itself hasn't gone away. I know it is there, every day. There are some days when it annoys me; others when it is almost imperceptible. Some days it makes me sad; occasionally it makes me laugh. But OCD is not in the driving seat of my life anymore. It has become the passenger I don't remember offering a lift to. There are still times when I would dearly love to throw it out of the car altogether. There are other days when OCD makes a bid to clamber into the front and wrestle control of the car from me. But the core principles of CBT do work: if you stick to them, and don't take any shortcuts, it will go back in its rightful place (sometimes quickly, other times after a little while). There really doesn't seem to be any other way to deal with that annoying passenger besides acceptance; I have tried lots of alternatives, thinking that they might somehow offer an alternative solution. I have sometimes tried to deny its existence, for example, which is completely counter-productive and very tiring. I have also tried to bargain with it: 'in return for some peace of mind, I'll adhere to your demands'. But, in the long term, that doesn't work either. Whatever respite I have ever been able to gain from these kinds of coping strategies has always been painfully temporary.

There are definitely times when I get angry that OCD 'happened' to me. But in my experience, the 'why me?' questions are always the most difficult to answer. After the diagnosis, I spent hours trying to figure it out. The only conclusion I have ever been able to reach is that some pretty bad things happen to just about everyone.

But there are things that have happened because of the OCD which have changed my life for the better. I mentioned earlier that the love and support I received from my wife and my family has been monumental. I was very lucky that throughout all of this I had the most supportive people around me that anyone could hope for – supportive in the sense that they bought into the concepts behind CBT and didn't let me revert back to my old ways of coping. Instead, they actively encouraged me to try to get better, and somehow managed to strike a balance between demonstrating love and affection and support for me, but resisting opportunities to try to help me drive the thoughts away. Quite how they did that – especially when I was at my most miserable – is difficult to imagine; it must have been very painful for them.

There have been times when the OCD frustrated all of us. And there are times when we have clashed about what represents the best way forward. But there has never been a moment when I doubted any of their support. That, probably more than anything, has been the key factor in my own attempts to get to grips with OCD.

There have been other positives, too. OCD has also given me a mental and emotional awareness that I lacked completely before. People are taught to take care of their bodies: don't overeat, don't drink too much and don't smoke too much, for example. There are annoying signs everywhere reminding us all about it. But it's less well-documented that your mind needs care and attention, too. And while I don't now spend my days in cross-legged meditation, stopping only to refocus my inner karma and nibble on a super fruit, I do acknowledge that the more you know about your mind, its strengths and weaknesses, and about what is important (and what is not) inside it, the better off you are likely to be.

One of the biggest eye-openers of the last four years has been how wide of the mark my initial perceptions of mental healthcare in the UK were. In all, I have probably shared details of my OCD with six or seven different professionals now. From the very first doctor I saw to the NHS psychiatrist and all the various CBT therapists, all have been sympathetic and easy to talk to. And most importantly of all, none of them has ever been visibly shocked or horrified by the things I have told them about the contents of my thoughts. Even if they have not been the right person to treat me themselves, they have pointed me in the direction of others who are.

People talk about there still being a stigma attached to mental illness. My experience has been the opposite. The people I have told about my OCD – including friends and colleagues – have, almost without exception, been supportive. Most can sympathize with the concept. Some even recognize and acknowledge that they themselves experience thoughts they would rather not have. In fact, the more I spoke to people about OCD, the more I began to see that almost everyone can usually relate to some kind of intrusive thought. The thought that you might jump in front of a train as it roars past you on the platform is, for some reason, pretty common. Less commonly told is the thought that you might push someone else in front of the train instead, but that's pretty well known, too, it seems.

For some people, it is a revelation when they discover that other people have these thoughts, and that they don't know what to do with them either. The insights I got from conversations like these were enormously valuable in benchmarking what are normal human experiences. They were also great in breaking down the sense of loneliness I have felt at many stages in the last four years.

Arguably, dealing with OCD has also given me a drive in my life that I almost certainly lacked before. I now want to get on with the rest of it. I have a desire back to do many of the same things that other people want to do. For so long it felt as though I didn't have any choices in my life. I couldn't plan for the future until I had dealt with my OCD, I felt. As a result, I effectively put my life on hold for a few years. And now I have it back again. I want to be a better husband; I want a family; I want to be a good father; I want a successful career. Achieving all of these things will doubtless bring with it challenges. And the OCD will almost certainly make its presence felt along the way. But that's no reason not to do it, I have grown to realize.

A partner's perspective

We had been together for about seven years when it happened. My boyfriend (as he was then) had always been a lively and sociable person, although that is not to say that he didn't occasionally have a bad mood or lose his temper! On the whole, his outlook was generally upbeat and positive. But over a period of only two or three weeks, he suddenly became very withdrawn, and uncharacteristically quiet. He didn't seem to be particularly engaged in what was going in our lives or with anyone around us. Quite often his mind seemed to be elsewhere, and he wouldn't necessarily answer questions I would ask him straightaway, as if he was somewhere else completely: it always seemed like he was concentrating on something inside his head.

He didn't seem to want to do any of the things we had previously enjoyed doing – he didn't seem to want to go out with friends, for example, and even lost interest in his football team (which did have its upsides: I got to watch something else on TV for once!). Physically, he seemed always to look tired and he seemed to see eating as a chore. He was losing weight quite quickly and starting to look less like himself.

At the time I had no idea what was going on, but I do remember thinking that it had to be more than just the shock and grief of the death of his colleague that was causing this change in him. I felt powerless and ineffective – like a child in some way, wanting an 'adult' to take over and tell us what the problem was ... I started to look on the internet into all sorts of ways of helping to lift his mood, by improving our diets, doing exercise, cutting down on alcohol and so on. He went to see the GP and then a friend recommended a therapist, and he went to see her, too. That definitely felt like a positive thing to do: it made me feel like we were being proactive in trying to find a solution. Then, after he was diagnosed, being led by a trained professional definitely gave me the confidence that he would inevitably get better. I started to feel hope that there was a way out for him ...

OCD has undoubtedly been the hardest issue we have had to face in our otherwise happy lives together. In some ways, the diagnosis was a relief even if only because this thing which had gripped him had a name, it meant that others must have it and that it must be treatable. At the beginning I had no feeling for how long it could take for him to get better – it seemed at certain stages like it might not happen for years. I definitely saw a marked improvement when he started the CBT and remember feeling hopeful then. But when there was a double dip later on I did wonder if he would ever be himself again.

The thoughts that he has occasionally sound horrible but they have never made me feel scared of him. I never thought that he would pick up a knife and stab me with it, for example. So I didn't have a problem being a part of some of the exposure exercises his therapist encouraged. Looking back, the only thing that scared me was that we might not be able to lead 'normal' lives because of the OCD.

The worst bit has been not being able to really do anything apart from be there for him; I couldn't quite believe that there wasn't more I could do. Watching him become a shell of the person he had been was really difficult and emotionally draining, and watching our families witness this decline in him was awful.

I know that for his parents and mine, it was incredibly hard to see him in such a desperate place; to begin with we were faced with something none of us knew much, if anything, about with no obvious solution. I had only ever come across the hoarding type of OCD and couldn't really understand how the thoughts he was having could cause him so much distress and anxiety. But reading the books and doing some internet research of my own helped to understand why and how the problem comes about, and gave me some insight into what was going through his head. The more I read, and the more I thought about it myself, the more I began to see that I sometimes get similar thoughts myself; I just don't give them a second thought. They don't cause me any problems, but recognizing that I have them helped to understand what can happen in the mind of an OCD sufferer, at least to some extent.

The best bit has been seeing him get back to being the person he was, seeing the hope return to his eyes. Since he was first diagnosed with OCD we have grown closer, got married and he is definitely in a different place now. It is obvious he still has the thoughts and that every once in a while they get him down, but on the whole he is able to manage them and experience them without getting distressed or depressed about them. He seems to want to look into the future much more than he did: he believes he can live with OCD without it consuming him entirely. At various points it seemed he might never feel like that. I have begun to take the improvement for granted, but watching him enjoy life again has been amazing. It almost makes up for the low points.

One of the positives is that we are definitely now a stronger unit, having come through this together. We appreciate the other more than we would have done if we had not had this hurdle – we definitely argue far less than we used to! It is a great relief for me that we are now able to make plans for our future, that there is one to look forward to and that he seems to want to take part in life again.

At really low points he would often ask 'Why me? . . . Why us? . . . What have we done to deserve this?' There is no answer to those questions. In some ways, what he has gone through has made us understand each other more and made us more grateful for what we do have together. Our families have definitely become more open and vocal about feelings and emotional and mental health than ever before!

OCD is definitely still there, but it is in the wings, not in the front row like it was a few years ago – I don't hate it or resent it as I did but just accept it as part of the person that I love . . . I still occasionally have to stop myself from being impatient or irritable with him when he is having a decline or low period. When things are tough, I try to make sure that we do what we can to make him concentrate on the real things in his life, and to get out of his head: we run more, try to eat more healthily . . .

OCD will probably rear its head several times more in our lives. I do feel though that we have got to a point where it doesn't rule his mind (and our lives) and it will not stop him experiencing a full, 'normal' life.

If I was to advise someone else in the same position as me, I would say that seeking medical professional help is, of course, really important, but also don't be afraid to be open-minded about trying alternative approaches like meditation (which we have recently started doing and seems to help him in some small way), yoga and running. Now that I know a little more about living with someone with mental health issues, I feel less scared by the whole thing – so I would say research as much as you can, go along to appointments if appropriate and keep positive.

A parent's viewpoint

With our son working and living in London and us living miles away, we gradually became aware that all was not well, without knowing precisely why. Certainly his telephone calls to us became more emotional and distressing for him (and for us). During a weekend when we were in London with him, he was obviously struggling to cope with everyday life and conversation. He tried to explain what he was experiencing and the only analogy we could think of was a computer with poisonous unwanted pop-ups that he was trying very hard to delete but couldn't.

He was extremely upset when we left that weekend and was clearly not coping well, much to our distress, too. He was convinced that he had a serious mental health problem – even more serious than it actually transpired to be. He became sure that he had schizophrenia and frequently mentioned the possible need to be sectioned.

When his GP referred him to a psychiatrist, he was diagnosed with OCD and secondary depression. He was told that what he had was as similar to schizophrenia as the common cold is to cancer. This statement started to put things into perspective and a measure of relief hove over the horizon for all of us, although it was not a solution in itself. We were still left wondering what had happened to our wonderful son, a great chap with a promising future ahead of him. What had we done during his childhood to cause this in later life? We felt it must be our fault. It was very easy to assign huge importance to insignificant past events and get things out of proportion.

We felt it was not up to us to talk about his problems to our friends – that was his prerogative – but when we did, to a couple of very close friends, it was a huge relief. We weren't ashamed – we just didn't know what had happened to him. We were desperate to find out the real problem and somehow be able to help him.

When our son came to live at home for several months we began to find out more about it, having not previously heard of OCD. He was referred by our local GP to a cognitive behaviour therapist and we read the same books that the therapist recommended to him. At a day-to-day level, he and his dad spent time rebuilding a wall in the garden. It had been on the 'to do' list for years but procrastination had triumphed. It was a strenuous work and this seemed to be quite useful as he could slowly become absorbed in physical activity with a purpose and conversation. However, it became clear after prolonged silences that he was ruminating again – thinking deeply over and over again about the problems in his mind – and needed to be further engaged in something.

At first, it seemed that the CBT was an inordinately slow process – the therapist and the books seemed to limit one's rate of progress unnecessarily. I still don't quite understand why an intelligent sufferer cannot work a bit faster through the chapters once the condition is diagnosed.

We found it quite difficult to strike the balance between providing support, which we wanted to do, and giving comfort, which could be construed as a coping strategy that the books and the therapist warned against. I joined a couple of the sessions with the therapist, which I found really useful in advising us how to help. As our son's treatment developed into exposure to the things which worried him, I think we understood the philosophy better. We were concerned when he had to undertake things which he clearly found very disturbing but did, I think, understand the logic.

For me, his mother, this was excruciating as I ached to comfort him in his distress and I tried to compromise by being constructive as well, but when your son tells you he can't face living any longer, it is agonizing; you feel so helpless and ineffectual, worrying about what he might do to himself, but hoping desperately that he won't carry out any of the awful things going on in his feverish brain. You know in your head and heart that he is not, and never could be, a murderer – of himself or anyone else.

We always had reservations about the SSRIs (selective serotonin reuptake inhibitors) which were prescribed by the first London psychiatrist he went to see, though we knew nothing initially about this form of medication. The internet provided useful information here and it seemed to be something which had to be tried. When he had made some progress, he decided that he should and could return to London, to work, to his girlfriend and to his other friends.

There was no instant fix, however. He came home again when he felt he couldn't cope, much to his poor girlfriend's dismay, but slowly he gained control again and it has been so heartening to watch him fight back. He also started consulting a different therapist and we were relieved when the first thing that he did was to get rid of the medication.

In some ways we were more fortunate than others. As our local GP said to me, 'At least he wants to succeed,' which made us realize that some people, faced with the enormity of OCD, just give up. It is so important for the sufferers and their families to know that the beastly thing can be brought under control, with the help of CBT. It would have been a huge help to us to know this at the time. Without that, it was a constant gnawing feeling of pain at his suffering that seemed interminable.

Gradually, we noticed our son gaining greater confidence in his ability to deal with life. Some days were better than others, inevitably, and we held our breath when he suffered a downturn, in case it became a nosedive, but CBT is an amazing process that really yields results, if you can keep disciplining yourself.

Probably the greatest proof of his success was that he

and his wonderful girlfriend got married last year. We were so proud of him and all that he had achieved as it is such a lonely path he has to follow when he is having to manage the beastly OCD. It was a wonderful event, enjoyed by all and when, during his speech, he spoke about his problems and how his now wife had always been 'the light at the end of the tunnel' it was enough to make anyone weep with happiness and pride!

Since that time, with our son in London and married, we inevitably know less about the specifics of his treatment. Indeed, we understand that part of that treatment is that he shouldn't continuously be talking about it. As a result we are very much in the background but usually have a suspicion when things are not as good as they might be. We know that he has great support from his wife, his psychiatrist and his friends. Most especially he has a determination not to let this thing beat him.

We know the problems with OCD will persist and that times of stress will exacerbate it, so are always anxious about the way in which he will be affected by events in his life. It is wonderful to know that he has done so well at work that he has been asked to undertake a brave new venture overseas. Although that brings problems, we are really pleased that his firm thinks so well of him. We feel he has a really good chance of leading a full and happy life with his wife (despite setbacks from time to time.) Thank goodness – a few years ago we thought that would be impossible.

Have we noticed any changes in our son's character? He has always been a very affectionate, loving and caring chap and that has not changed at all. If anything, the OCD has brought us closer, particularly his relationship with his father. We are more conscious of possible problems and are probably more protective of him than before and more vulnerable to his mood swings. What I think has changed is that coming to his childhood home is bitter-sweet now as he spent some months of misery here, battling with OCD, and the house can only remind him of that. However, there are happy memories, too, which help.

We have both learnt a lot more about mental illness, and the facilities and people available for those suffering. I think we are a lot more receptive to their problems and defend sufferers if others poke fun or are dismissive.

2

It's only dirt

Only a couple of years ago my hands were raw and cracked from continuous washing. I say my hands, but really I should say my arms as everything up to my elbow was dried out and unsightly, not to mention sore. They'd been that way for years. I couldn't remember the last time I'd worn a T-shirt or short-sleeved dress. I hated summer because it was more difficult to hide them. You'd think that would be enough to get me to stop doing it, to change, but it wasn't. Although I knew my washing was excessive and ridiculous, that didn't change anything. I just couldn't stop. I guess a small part of me believed that I was right about dirt and everyone else was wrong. The desire to keep everything clean and keep those around me safe was too strong and I just didn't seem to be able to break the washing habit. In the end it was the thought of having my fiancé hold my dry, cracked, ugly hands on my wedding day that finally made me seek help. Imagine trying to put a ring on that hand! I couldn't bear the shame of having all my friends and family see me as a bride with my ugly, damaged skin, not to mention the fact that I was having trouble finding a nice wedding dress with long sleeves!

Perhaps my reasons for finally seeking help sound a little shallow. I should explain what was really going on – it wasn't only my hands and arms that were suffering. My fiancé, with whom I lived, was subjected not only to rules and regulations about taking off his shoes and only putting his bag in certain places but, worse than that, the idea of him holding or touching our baby girl before he'd showered and changed (to make himself safe in my eyes) was too much for me to bear. I told myself that it wasn't a big deal and that I was behaving just as any new mother did and that I was right to be cautious: after all, I had to protect our baby – that was my greatest responsibility in life. My fiancé was pretty good at doing what I asked, or rather insisted, in order to keep the peace, but I knew he was getting increasingly unhappy and frustrated about my behaviour. We began to argue about it and coupled with the lack of sleep from having a small child, despite our impending wedding, the cracks in our relationship were beginning to show as clearly as the cracks in my hands.

One morning I went into the kitchen after my fiancé had left for work to find a book on the table. It was about getting over OCD. I knew about OCD and if I'm honest I knew I probably had it but I wasn't ready to admit it to myself. I still hid behind the idea that I was being careful, that I was protecting my family and myself. The idea of doing anything differently terrified me. Just thinking about my daughter coming into contact with germs that I could and should protect her from was enough for me to start sweating, then my heart would start racing. Surely if it caused this much anxiety I must be right – there was real danger that needed to be avoided. The first thing I did when I saw the book on the kitchen table (our kitchen table where not only we, but also our baby, ate!) was to get an antibacterial wipe. I picked up the book and wiped the table down, and then I wiped the book down with a new wipe before replacing it on the table. Phew, it was clean now. I threw the wipes away and started washing my hands. Where had he got that book? Had he bought it in a bookshop? If so what kind of germs would it have on it? The sales assistant might have been ill or maybe they were a student who didn't bother to wash their hands after going to the loo? Worse still he might have borrowed it from someone – it could have been touched by tens, maybe hundreds of people . . . imagine how many germs that would be . . .

As these thoughts rattled through my head I stood at the sink, aimlessly looking out the window and scrubbing. Yes, scrubbing. I didn't just wash my hands with soap and water, oh no. I had a scrubbing brush by every sink and a distinct method of washing my hands and arms so I couldn't overlook any part of the process. If I forgot where I'd got to or was interrupted by the phone (which I didn't pick up) or something else I would have to start over – just to be on the safe side. After all, in twenty minutes my daughter would be waking from her nap and I'd be picking her up, feeding her, playing with her, so my hands *needed* to be properly clean. When I'd finished I turned back to the kitchen table and looked at the book. Perhaps I should at least try, for my fiancé's sake. There was a note inside. It said, 'I love you and I'm here for you but we can't go on living like this. You need to do something to help yourself.' I was horrified (although glad he said he still loved me): had it really got that bad for him?

I read the book. It was the least I could do. At first I was relieved to understand that I wasn't the only person who had problems like mine. I wasn't weird or crazy. I started to understand that the problem was not one of actual contamination, but of thoughts about contamination. To overcome the problem, the book described different techniques called 'exposure and response prevention', which basically meant deliberately doing the thing that you get anxious about and then not doing anything to make yourself feel better about it. I soon discovered this was a lot easier said than done. I did *try* not to avoid the things I thought were dirty, but as soon as I became anxious about something I went straight back to my old ways. Weeks passed and I pacified my fiancé with the idea that I was trying to change.

The day my best friend and I went shopping for my wedding dress should have been lovely. At the start I managed to hide my hands behind my back enough to deceive myself that there wasn't a problem, but halfway through trying on a dress I broke down. All I could see in the mirror were my red raw arms and dry, split hands. It was then I realized I couldn't keep lying to myself anymore, the OCD was ruling and ruining my life in more ways than I'd let myself believe. So I took the plunge and went to see my GP. It was the first time I'd been to see her about this but I knew I wanted to ask for a referral to a CBT therapist as CBT was recommended as an effective treatment in the book I'd been reading.

Fortunately, my GP was able to refer me to a therapist who specialized in treating people with OCD on the NHS and, strangely, I was almost excited when I arrived for my first appointment. Finally someone was going to help me where I'd failed to help myself. The first few sessions were a revelation; to be able to talk freely to someone who really understood what I was going through, who didn't seem to think I was crazy and who reassured me that not only was OCD way more common than I'd ever thought, but more importantly that there was a way of beating it and changing for the better. Important concepts which I'd read in the book but forgotten soon after, such as the fact that just because I thought things were contaminated and needed cleaning it didn't necessarily mean they did, started to gradually sink in. My therapist repeatedly encouraged me to see that the problem was one of worry about contaminating those I loved, rather than a problem of actually contaminating them and that the more attention I paid to these worries, and the more I acted on them, the worse the problem became. Although it was difficult at first to accept and believe what she was saying, I couldn't really argue with the second part as I'd witnessed it happening to me over the years.

My fiancé was so pleased that I'd finally sought help and I was also feeling more positive because I felt I was 'doing something'. However, after about six sessions with the therapist he pointed out that he hadn't seen my actual behaviour change – I was still washing and scrubbing as much as I'd been before. Although I felt more confident because I was talking to my therapist about my OCD, in fact I'd been lying to myself and to my therapist about following her advice. We'd set up tasks in the session for me to deliberately expose myself, the house and our baby to some of the things that I found anxiety-provoking. We'd written a list of situations I found made me feel very anxious and the plan was to start at the bottom and work

my way up towards the most anxiety-provoking situations. My first task was simply to take the milk out of the
fridge and put it in different places on the kitchen work
surface and then not wash down the work surface afterwards. It probably sounds simple but I found it impossible to cope with the thought of all the germs so I quickly
cleaned the surface with an antibacterial wipe. Another
task was to pick up the post from the doormat and open
it all without washing my hands afterwards. It was just so
uncomfortable for me and the thought of contaminating
my baby was too much to bear. So after a few tears and
some reluctance on my part I agreed with my therapist
that we'd have some sessions at my house so that she
could demonstrate to me exactly how to do the exposure
exercises and then be there while I did them.

I hardly slept the night before our first session. I was
terrified about what my therapist was going to make me
do and that I'd never feel safe or comfortable in my own
home again. What if things were contaminated so much
that I could never get it to feel clean again? I voiced these
fears to my therapist over a cup of tea when she arrived
(my distraction tactic) and she reminded me that the idea
was not for things to feel clean and safe, but for them to
feel dirty and uncomfortable and to deal with this feeling
in a different way to how I'd been dealing with it up until
now. She had already explained in a previous session that
in situations where I feel anxious, my anxiety should
subside after a while even if I didn't do anything, such as
cleaning or washing, to make it go away. It was still very
hard to believe that that would really happen.

In practice, the exposure exercises were so much more
thorough than anything I'd dared to try on my own. For

example, when we'd agreed to contaminate the kitchen with an un-wiped packet of biscuits from the supermarket I thought I'd just have to put it on the side and leave it there for a bit and then put it away. How wrong I was. My therapist helped me to see that if I only did that it would be too easy for me to avoid that area and therefore I wouldn't get the full effect of the exposure. I was reminded again that the idea was for things to feel really dirty and contaminated so that I could then practise not acting out my compulsions such as cleaning and scrubbing or throwing away things I thought were contaminated. In this way, she explained, I would be teaching myself that even if things feel dirty and it's uncomfortable it's not the end of the world and the anxiety and discomfort will decrease after time and would hopefully go away altogether eventually.

So instead of just gingerly placing the biscuit packet in one place, my therapist first of all got me to touch the packet all over so that my hands felt really dirty. Then I had to roll the packet around not only the kitchen work surface but also in the drawers and cupboards (I know it sounds crazy and I did feel weird doing it!). The idea was to contaminate the kitchen so thoroughly that I would find it very difficult to wash everything down afterwards. Once I'd done this I wasn't allowed to wipe anything or wash my hands until my anxiety had subsided.

Amazingly, although I felt extremely anxious and uncomfortable to begin with as I was not able to go back and 'decontaminate' the areas I'd wiped, my anxiety did actually start to decrease. It ended up subsiding much quicker than I thought it would. It was very tough but having my therapist with me really helped and, unbelievably, my anxiety didn't stay really high for that long, maybe ten to fifteen minutes. After that I still felt anxious but it was at a more manageable level and therefore I was better able to resist my urge to wash and clean the kitchen and my hands and arms.

Over the coming weeks, as we continued to contaminate everything in the house and I had to challenge myself to do more exposure exercises. I was no longer allowed to have 'safe' places and I had to start allowing people to walk around the house with their shoes on. I had to take my supermarket shopping bags and put them on my bed. I had to contaminate the clean washing when I took it out of the machine, firstly with things that I found less anxiety-provoking such as groceries and then later with outdoor coats and even shoes. The list goes on. Just when I thought I was there my therapist would notice something else I was avoiding. I didn't do it on purpose, often I didn't even recognize it as being part of the OCD. Later, I was able to do the exposure exercises by myself. Interestingly, if I put off doing them in the morning I found it much more difficult to do them in the evening as it seemed to be easier to come up with excuses, such as feeling too tired or already having other plans. So, with encouragement from my therapist, I forced myself to contaminate things in the morning so that I was living with the discomfort during the day.

To be honest, I did really hate it at the beginning but after the first couple of weeks I began to notice my skin looking less ravaged, which made me feel good about myself and I think gave me the confidence to keep going. Not that I didn't still have setbacks. Three weeks into the process, when I was resisting washing my hands apart from before meals and after going to the toilet (my therapist did suggest I didn't wash them at all in order to prove to myself that even if I didn't wash my hands for several days my family would probably survive, but I couldn't go quite that far!), I had some kind of stomach bug, with sickness, diarrhoea, the lot. Was this the beginning of my worst fears? Had I gone too far in starting to allow people to walk in the house without taking their shoes off? What if my daughter caught it and died? It would be all my fault. I felt really panicky and as soon as I could find the energy I set about first of all decontaminating myself and then cleaning the house from top to bottom. I was convinced that if I made everything 'safe' my anxiety would go away and my daughter would be fine.

Strangely, halfway through the process, after I'd done the bathroom and kitchen, I realized that I was actually feeling even more anxious than when I started. Clearly it wasn't clean enough yet. I was still in a frenzy when my fiancé came home and I screamed at him to take his shoes off. Rather than agreeing he took me calmly by the hand and sat me down at the kitchen table and made me tell him what was wrong. I thought I could convince him that I had to continue my cleaning but he'd learnt a lot about how to deal with my OCD in the past months and he talked to me in the way my therapist had taught him – helping me see that this was just an extreme bout of anxiety and that illness was a normal part of life. He was so encouraging about all the progress I'd made that he somehow persuaded me that if I re-contaminated all the areas I'd just cleaned and got through this anxiety then I would be winning. It was the hardest thing I've ever done but with his support I did it, and eventually, slowly, the anxiety did subside.

It's hard to pinpoint exactly when my obsession with keeping things germ-free started. I remember having a nasty virus as a teenager and worrying that I might spread it to my friends and family if I wasn't careful and I started washing my hands more thoroughly and more regularly. However, it's easier to pinpoint the moment I realized that I was no longer a slave to OCD: my partner and daughter came in from the park and, before he'd a chance to stop her, my daughter had come toddling into the kitchen with her boots on and her hands full of 'gifts' she'd brought from the park: a feather, a knobbly stick, a pine cone, a leaf and a fair amount of earth to boot. She laid them out on the kitchen table and, swinging her little legs, proudly named them for me. I'd be lying if I said I didn't feel a surge of anxiety when she came in with her boots on clutching things she'd picked up from the ground, but then a funny thing happened. I was so caught up in her delight that I actually completely forgot about the dirt. I guess it had finally dawned on me that dirt really was just dirt and probably wasn't going to kill anyone. And frankly, it was worth the risk to be able to enjoy moments like this without feeling anxious and without cleaning and washing. With my therapist's voice ringing in my ears, saying 'do the opposite of what the OCD wants you to do', I reached for the biscuit jar and offered one to my daughter. She held up her grubby two-year-old hands.

'Dirty,' she said.

'That's OK, it's only dirt,' I replied.

3

Emerging from my private hell

I always had an obsession about the number three from a very young age. At first my obsession was more a fascination with any object or occurrence that came in threes, but eventually this obsession with the number three resulted in my development of actions and behaviour with the theme 'three times'. For example, I would whistle three times to make a bad thought or feeling go away. My parents were more amused than concerned with this behaviour and at times such as Christmas when the family was together, aunties and uncles laughed and recounted tales of whether to tread on or avoid the cracks in the pavement. It seemed that obsessive behaviour was either good for you or just a family trait!

Life moved on and I progressed from primary school to secondary school and became a teenager. I still experienced these thoughts, but they had evolved. Their focus was no longer just on the number three, but now included more sinister and intrusive themes and images, such as the death of my parents if I did not wait up for them to return home after an evening out. I worried about being orphaned and having to live in a children's home. I was disturbed by violent images of hurt and accidents happening to my wider family. I also worried about global catastrophes. With hindsight these evolving thoughts were fuelled by reading science fiction books and watching horror films. Notwithstanding this major hindrance, I successfully passed a solid clutch of GCSE equivalents and became a sixth-form student. By the end of the first year in sixth form, I was one of the top students at school with the potential to gain a place at a leading university.

However, my ongoing personal challenge was that one side of my personality seemed determined on making my life a misery, tiring and challenging; a hell on earth. My first memorable encounter with this personality trait was at Lincoln Castle, which we visited on a family holiday during one of those glorious hot and blue-sky summers of the 1970s. The unconsecrated prisoners' graveyard from the days when Lincoln Castle was a prison became a source of ruminations, anxiety and intrusive thoughts to me for many days. These thoughts ruined my family holiday as I became introverted and very thoughtful. But I knew better: I could cope, I could beat these intrusive thoughts – I began to neutralize them. If I thought of someone being harmed, I would then think of that harm happening to me instead, thereby protecting the other person. If anyone was going to be killed or mutilated it would be me. My belief was that logic and intelligence would overcome these intrusive thoughts and let me lead a normal life. After all, I was a top student with proven success and the potential to do well in academic life.

The university entrance examinations came and went, and then it was Christmas. My life moved into the new year with my favourite band, Queen, at number one with 'Bohemian Rhapsody'. I had achieved a scholarship at a university and life should have been good. However, there was always a 'but'. There was a noise inside my head and intrusive thoughts. I thought I could harm, even kill, my family and friends. I felt mental pain and intellectual paralysis. At Easter I saw a trailer for the film *The Exorcist* and then God and the Devil came in to my thoughts. I lasted less than a week before crying my heart out to my girlfriend and then my father. My father sought medical help for me.

I failed my A levels, my mother died and my world fell apart. I did receive medical help through psychiatry and was on Valium for two years. I did resit my A levels and again received poor results, but the university held my scholarship open for me. I went to university, could not cope, left and returned in mental disarray to live with my father and continue my relationship with a very understanding girlfriend who I eventually married and is still my wife. From academic glory and success, I went to being an office junior making the tea and undertaking the most basic of work duties. The intrusive thoughts did not ever stop but somehow drifted to the back of my mind and life began again. Somehow I survived, even thrived, and the decades passed by.

Then, in 2004, my father died.

This is when my story really starts.

By this time I was married, a family man with two brilliant kids and, in relative terms, I was a successful and senior person at work. When Dad died, it was quite natural that I should have feelings of sadness at the loss. We were close. I missed him and still do. I was at work when my wife telephoned me with the news of Dad's sudden heart attack and I rushed to his house to find him dead. I felt intense grief and loss – like a hole of despair had opened up in my life. At my father's house that day, my life in some ways returned to the 1970s. My story is not about the amazing 1970s – hot summers, the miners' strike, Harold Wilson, the Sex Pistols and, of course, Queen. I experienced intrusive thoughts again that I had not had since later in that decade. The mental pain came back and I began to dwell on these intrusive thoughts.

With reflection my life up until my father's death had not been perfect. There had been issues in my work environment in terms of being passed over on the promotion ladder. While I had been pragmatic in my handling of ongoing changes at work, I suspect that these changes impacted adversely on my confidence and well-being. I was also very busy and maybe I was not as much of a husband and father as I should have been, particularly as my children were in their teenage years. So perhaps my mental instability was not just all about my father's death but also reflected pressures in the workplace and at home.

During 2005 I noticed that I was not feeling quite right. This feeling is hard to exactly pinpoint as it was a gradual deterioration in the way I was thinking. I do not think anyone noticed this deterioration in me at the time – indeed, even my wife was unaware of it until I sought medical help in 2007. I remember feeling in the meantime that I would never feel happy again and that I no longer looked forward to living my life. I worried a lot and needed to keep thinking through details to put my mind at rest. Decision-making took longer and required more reasoning, together with internal mental debate. I had lost the ability to think naturally. I gradually began to feel more exhausted as the year went by, as well as generally unhappy as if something bad was sitting on my shoulder or overlooking my life.

However, life was not all doom and gloom, and I hid these intrusive thoughts by throwing myself into work. I tried to use my seniority and responsibility as tools to bring myself back to earth – to manage my thinking through sound logic and reasoning. I felt that I knew exactly what was wrong in my own mind; the thoughts were back from my childhood. I did not seek professional help as, after all, I had survived the first bout of intrusive thoughts all those years ago. To seek professional help also felt potentially embarrassing in my position. I did feel alone, but I was confident that I had enough knowledge and experience to sort myself out.

As I moved into 2006, I felt that my strategy was working. I had stabilized my worrying and I was aware of the dangers of excessive ruminations. I felt that I had made significant progress and I had turned the corner. Then I ended up having a horrendous accident involving a severely broken arm and major ongoing surgery that lasted two years. It was only a simple matter of falling over in the garden but I fell on a tree root and my arm snapped, with one bone broken in four places.

As I waited for medical help to arrive at the scene, I was rational, asking my wife to pack a book and other basic items for me. I was trying to manage my hospitalization in a positive way, rather than being a victim. The medics put me on morphine and then in hospital I was prescribed morphine-based pain medication. As the first operation was not a success and my arm remained broken, I ended up remaining on strong pain medication for a long time. While I felt secure in the hospital ward I did have a sense of foreboding as if something bad was building up in me. This fear became reality when I was showering by myself on day three of my hospitalization; unexpectedly, I was confronted with all the worse thoughts of my childhood: the death of a family member, the hurting and mutilation of individuals, the Devil versus God, but with thirty years of enhancement. The thoughts had become more real, graphic and terrifying from a personal perspective. These intrusive thoughts could not be ignored or left alone; they needed my intervention through neutralization. It was a shocking moment; all my mind wanted to do was neutralize, neutralize and neutralize. I felt terrible and looked terrible but I felt unable to talk to any of the nursing staff about how I was feeling. I felt guilty and embarrassed, and still wanted to sort my thoughts out myself. I was fearful of how horrible my thoughts were.

After four days I was discharged from hospital and went home, still with a feeling of general unease; something 'not right' sat on my shoulder; a shadow, something dark, was there in my mind and worrying. I was not at peace with myself and could not relax and enjoy life. On the Friday my work colleagues came to my home and took me down to a local pub for lunch. While it was good to see the team, and I welcomed their company, I felt anxious and not relaxed. It was not a good feeling but I accepted that I was on strong pain management medication and my feelings were probably influenced by the tablets.

I went to bed that night exhausted but reconciled my intrusive thoughts on the basis that I had suffered a major accident and had undergone major surgery.

I continued to feel bad in myself; it is difficult to clarify, but there was an overall feeling of unease, blackness and lack of enthusiasm for life. I saw no future and ruminated about the past, and seemed to become focused on the 1970s in the period before the thoughts came into my life: a time when my mind felt calm and I felt happy and content in myself. None of my thoughts made sense. I had no sense of place; I felt lost and bewildered. I had no counsel because I felt unable to tell my wife; I was unable to talk or confide in anyone. I felt absolutely awful.

After I was discharged from hospital, my ruminations had begun to accelerate and evolve. The basic routines of washing, brushing teeth and even putting in my contact lenses became elongated and ritualistic. I was ruminating and ritualizing, and life became hell on earth again. Interestingly enough, the worse trigger related to a television documentary about the 1970s, which I was viewing at home on the Saturday night after my accident.

Close friends were coming round for supper to see me and my wife had left me 'pillowed up' in front of the television as I was on strong medication and with a plaster cast. While I am unsure whether I believe in coincidences, the documentary was about the band Queen and the production of the album *A Night at the Opera*. The documentary focused on the number one single that came from this album: 'Bohemian Rhapsody'. Band members Brian May and Roger Taylor revisited the building where the band had recorded the song in 1975. The documentary was fascinating and nostalgic, but it evoked meaningful and heart-rending memories of my childhood and growing up as a teenager. My reasoning told me that this was not right; not wrong, but just not right. My thoughts needed a sense of perspective and logic, but this was not to be – suddenly I became lost in my 'world of 1970s'. I was looking to escape to the time of my life before the thoughts began. I knew that this was destructive but, despite all my historical mental disciplines, I remained lost in my past, with historical intrusive thoughts invading my mind and life. While mentally I could return to the 1970s, a time when life was simple and uncomplicated, I could not apply the lessons learnt then to my life now.

As usual I remained calm and kept my pain to myself for eighteen months. I had been through these intrusions before and thought that, as a senior individual in the business sector, I could fight them with common sense and logical reasoning.

I was in continual pain as the arm did not heal and remained broken in four places. I remained on heavy duty pain relief for multiple fractures. The self-doubt and concern worsened together with the increasing need to ruminate on my thoughts. I was faced with the need to neutralize my thoughts.

I wear contact lenses during the day. With a broken arm, the actual procedure of placing contact lenses to each eye is not easy or straightforward at best. The first time I decided to treat myself to the luxury of contact lenses rather than spectacles, it took me thirty minutes until I was successful. For an individual with one arm in a plaster cast from his thumb to his shoulder, completing this procedure should have been something of a victory. But no. My mind evoked the 'devil eyes' of someone who could hurt others, so I felt the need to remove my hard-won contact lenses to neutralize this worrying, intrusive thought and begin again.

The ruminating and neutralizing became more constant. For example, if I thought of Lucifer then the neutralizing thought process was 'luminous, lord saviour, lord almighty'; a bad thought turned to good. However, this process of neutralization could take more than three attempts and sometimes I could not dismiss the thoughts. As time went on the intrusive thoughts multiplied. It became mentally painful trying to watch television or listen to music. All I longed for was to have a clear mind and silence in my head. Instead, I was suffering from the mental pain of frightening intrusive thoughts that I wanted to continually neutralize. This created ongoing concern, worry and anxiety.

I lost part of my grip on the real world, particularly my family life. My main focus remained work as, with hindsight, work was more detached from the 'real world'. Day-to-day life had become difficult; I could not focus or concentrate on reality.

I did telephone my GP for help but did not tell the truth. I explained that I was suffering from anxiety and tension; while this was true, I did not expand on the intrusive thoughts and the need to neutralize. My doctor prescribed medication to calm me down by reducing anxiety – a 'green pill', as I remember.

I had to wait for the whole first half of 2006 for major surgery to save my arm. The anaesthetic was a welcome relief as for the first time in months my mind switched off. But like all good things, it came to an end and I woke up to reality. While the operation was ultimately a success, it was not without complications. These necessitated three more operations. In the interim, particularly during 2007, I remained on strong medication to manage the pain.

During the summer of 2006, while I was recovering from the major surgery, part of me felt better, but slowly and surely the doubt and darkness came back into my life.

The ruminations and the need to neutralize seemed to kick-start and my logic failed. As the year ended I was under intense pressure at work and the family was growing up in terms of studying for GCSEs and A levels. There was a lot going on and I was struggling to focus.

However, in a covert way, I did seek help for the first time. My employer offered a psychological counselling service on a confidential basis for stress at work and general home- or life-related concerns. I did telephone the counselling helpline and confessed to concerns and worries relating to my operations as well as the general feeling of loss of my childhood; a temporal kick back in time. The employer's counselling service was caring and helpful; after two telephones assessments, I was offered six face-to-face meetings of one hour with a psychologist, paid for by my employer. My broken arm was still in plaster at the time and I remained on pain medication.

The counselling was helpful and supportive, and helped me survive the next major operation. But this support only calmed my problems – in fairness to the counsellor, I did not inform them of my real concerns: the disturbing and violent, intrusive thoughts. The face-to-face support was followed by an ongoing telephone counselling service every week, but I continued to limit the information in terms of how I felt and the intrusive thoughts I was experiencing.

In 2007, I began to ritualize on a regular basis, which was all about taking the intrusive thought and basically making myself the victim of my thoughts of death or violence. If I could be satisfied that the only person to be hurt was me then eventually I could dismiss the intrusive thought and calm myself down. My logic failed to put my mind at rest. As I have mentioned, when I was a child I was worried about the number three and the potential impact of not neutralizing by doing an activity such as thinking about a thought three times. The number three suddenly became meaningful and important again in my life, and I needed to neutralize each intrusive thought at least three times. 'Hell on earth' was back with a vengeance.

My work life was hectic and pressurized, and there was a lot going on in day-to-day living. The intrusive thoughts got even worse and more intense. The thoughts were all around me, triggered by many prompts. The more intense the thoughts became, the more I wanted to put more effort and time into neutralizing them. My sense of foreboding and of a black shadow became worse and I lost the joy of living. I only ever considered suicide once – it was just after another operation and I was still on pain medication.

I was eighteen months into this mental trauma but still working and living life. We had a major family holiday in the summer of 2007, exploring remote parts of Africa. I was only just functioning, but to the outside world, including to my wife and children, I appeared to be fine. No one witnessed or experienced my ruminations and rituals. However, the personal impact of this illness was worsening as my rituals became more complex and required more repetition of the activity I was undertaking at the time of the thought. For example, I would drive past the location where I had experienced an intrusive thought at least three times to neutralize my concern; simple acts had become major events and took up a lot of my time. My journey to work of six miles could increase by three or four miles as I drove up and down to neutralize. Perhaps not surprisingly, in myself I was becoming tired and irritable. Friends and colleagues had noticed that I had become forgetful and distracted.

The turning point was a Sunday evening in the summer of 2007 when I had a drink at a local pub with my wife, son and his friend. My wife, son and I returned home for an evening meal and I was sat at the table ruminating. My wife commented that as usual I was not listening to her and asked what the problem was; I explained that I was feeling mentally unwell but promised to seek help. When I had first met my wife in 1977, I had talked through the problems that I experienced a year earlier. I explained that I had suffered a nervous breakdown through too much studying but provided little detail as to what I suffered from. My wife was aware that I was sensitive to religious places, for example, perhaps without really understanding why.

In a sense my wife and I left the issue at that. On the next day I telephoned the medical helpline at work again, explained how I felt and tried to talk through the intrusive thoughts. I felt embarrassed and awkward. However, it was a constructive conversation and I did open up to the medical adviser, who suggested that I should speak to my doctor. I felt empowered to sort out my illness. I telephoned my doctor but was advised by the surgery receptionist that I would have to wait at least two working days for an appointment. When I explained why I needed to see my doctor, the receptionist advised me to contact a twenty-four-hour mental health crisis management team.

The team was caring and supportive. I met a team member for an initial interview to assess my needs and was then referred to a psychiatrist. This was now autumn and initially I refused the offer of being signed off work with depression, and instead worked on until November. However, with hindsight I realize that the new medication I was given made my mental condition worse, as I lost the little ability I had left to exercise logic. The medication made me weary and mentally sluggish, which prevented me from tackling the intrusive thoughts through reasoned thoughts. I was feeling spaced out and as a result the neutralization took longer to achieve. My mental well-being went downhill and worsened after another operation on my arm, which necessitated more strong pain medication.

I was diagnosed by the psychiatrist as being depressed and was provided with caring support by the local team of nurses. I had regular meetings with the team and was given further support at various times when living had become too much for me. There was also exposure work when team members would pick me up at home and take me to a local church to face my fears about good and evil. From my perspective, the support was robust and there for me, for which I will always be grateful. The team consisted of a great bunch of individuals who genuinely tried to help me. Everyone in the team tried their best to keep me from hospitalization.

Again with the benefit of hindsight, my main need was to talk through my feelings and concerns. There was unfortunately a long waiting list to meet a consultant psychologist and for the first month I just talked to the team and the psychiatrist. However, I had private medical insurance through work and eventually went to see a psychologist on a private basis. While there was some concern expressed by the team at first, my decision was accepted and for a month I was supported by both the hospital and by a private psychologist.

The private psychologist suggested that I may actually be suffering from OCD: obsessive compulsive disorder. For that month I received two treatments: psychiatry and medication together with psychological counselling. Both treatments involved exposure work; for example, my private psychologist suggested that I actually watch a DVD of *The Exorcist*. My wife was there for me and we did work together to try and overcome this condition. She supported me in my exposure work and joined most of the hospital and private consultations that took place from September to November 2007.

However, by December my condition had worsened and the psychiatrist recommended a course of six sessions of electroconvulsive therapy (ECT). My wife undertook extensive research of this treatment as from a media perspective it has a dramatic image. My private psychologist was appalled and advised against such a course of treatment. I was told that if I went ahead with this option, my private treatment would end as it would be pointless. However, I was desperate and agreed to try it. My wife made it clear to the psychiatrist that if there was no improvement in my mental health during the treatment that she would ask for a referral elsewhere. The ECT was carried out and my mental health deteriorated. For the first time in my life I felt suicidal. I could not think clearly, I was becoming a recluse; I was in mental pain. I welcomed sleep and would take any combination of alcohol and medication to 'close down' for the night.

My wife had researched OCD on the internet and had found the link to the OCD UK charity. My wife contacted the helpline and was referred to a leading OCD specialist in the UK. He spoke to my wife directly and after talking through my symptoms arranged to meet me at a private psychiatric hospital specializing in OCD. I was admitted as a patient for four weeks during which a medical recovery programme was initiated.

An important factor in terms of my recovery is that my wife supported me during this difficult time. After talking through the implications with me, she confided in a close friend. Our friend was supportive and understanding. She helped organize my hospitalization, joined us during the admission process and was there for my wife throughout my hospitalization. Likewise, she helped compile case notes and a history of my condition to support my admission. While it was embarrassing at first to talk about my history, she was objective and kind, and I was able to talk openly. The important point and lesson is that my wife was not alone and could talk about her concerns and worries to an impartial friend. The learning point to me is that the OCD sufferer can become very introverted and very selfish. The focus is you and not the people in the background who are affected by your behaviour and illness.

It is very difficult for the wider population of family and friends who are involved with your OCD. These individuals often need support, but particularly need an understanding of your condition and actions. Likewise, work and employment can be an issue. I was fortunate to have a very understanding boss who was there for me and was very reassuring for my wife. However, I am sure that this is not always the case. I was very honest with my boss and he facilitated a phased return to work and refused to talk to anyone who asked him what was wrong with me. My boss was steadfast in his support.

My colleagues and friends were as equally as support-ive. They were there for me to talk to and update regard-ing work and life, but never intruded into my illness. I was embarrassed and felt foolish and vulnerable. There was a senior work event during the third week of my hospital-ization and my boss asked me to join the team for a catch-up and drink. I got the medical OK and spent a very enjoyable three hours or so with colleagues, who again just talked to me and made me feel welcome. I have since talked about my experience to a male colleague over a Chinese meal and a beer. He did not press but I felt better in myself talking through the bad times of 2007. It was 'good to talk' but you do need to be careful and think about your audience!

In my view, my children had a hard time although our son was particularly supportive and we have talked very openly since (he is studying medicine at university). My daughter probably found her dad a bit weird, particularly when I was neutralizing bad thoughts by staring at her for long period of times as I moved the hurt from her to me. But, again, as a family they were caring and during a family holiday we made the effort to visit the private psychiatric hospital to show the kids where Dad had stayed. I learnt that relative openness and honesty with the people you love does help the recovery. These individ-uals do need some understanding and involvement. My wife's parents were also very supportive as well as my wife's grown-up niece.

Throughout my treatment I have asked my wife to be with me whenever possible; it's not easy for either of us, but she needs to know. This has also given my wife, with the support of her friend, the strength, insight and knowledge to help me. My wife is also fully aware of my ongoing medication and psychological support. My years of silence have been superseded with openness and involvement including seeing the drafts of this article.

I accept that I am fortunate in that I was able to have access to private medical care and ongoing support over the past two years. But to misquote the infamous Monty Python's *Life of Brian* – 'what has the specialist hospital ever done for me?!' Well for a start the specialist spoke directly with my wife, listened, met me and diagnosed my condition. I was admitted into a caring environment where I met people with similar problems and with OCD. It helped just to talk to other people and understand that I was not alone in the way I felt. I was also living in a secure environment where I was encouraged to talk about my feelings as well as given the opportunity to experience exposure to my concerns. I was encouraged to go out into the wide world, and my wife and I stayed at a local hotel every weekend to be together. My wife also actively supported my exposure to my fears and thoughts, working with the hospital and psychologists. It was very much a team effort.

I think, however, that the most important aspect of this support related to medication. The medication for depression seemed to make my condition worse as the drugs blunted my ability to reason and use logic to face up to my illness. My medication was radically changed over the month that I was in hospital – the more suitable, reduced medication meant that my mind was clearer, and this helped my recovery. With the help of others, I was now able to let my own mind work towards overcoming OCD. You need to fight and overcome OCD through strength of mind, learning to ignore intrusive thoughts and move on in your life. I found that all the medication for depression did was to blunt the anxiety at best: only you can make the thoughts go away through challenging them.

OCD is a bully that preys on your every weakness and doubt. The only way to tackle a bully is to stand up for yourself: tackle the hurt in a measured and sensible way; involve people and ask for help and support. I can promise anyone reading this book that I understand the need to neutralize and ritualize but the sooner you stop and live with your thoughts, the sooner you will be on the road to recovery. These are no small words – it is tough, hard and emotional. Resistance does work but, in the process, this stance can take you through a private hell and back.

Intrusive thoughts and the need to ritualize can be immediate or take many years to come into your life. Letting go is hard and difficult. OCD is addictive and a real illness that most people do not understand or recognize.

Openness and honesty are the starting points and, I suspect, sheer strong will. To tackle the challenge of OCD, to start with you need to wake up one day and say to yourself 'enough'. Then live your life as a normal human being. Unfortunately life is never that simple and the mind will not give you the logical option. However, you can decide to get relevant help and work through the issues. OCD is a terrible illness that hurts many of us but, like many illnesses, it can be overcome. The first stage in tackling OCD is to recognize that you are not well in yourself and to seek help and guidance.

We all have different journeys in tackling OCD and varied techniques. My own experience would recommend the need to keep a clear head; to manage yourself in terms of rest and relaxation by avoiding extremes in terms of busy days and late nights; to be careful about your alcohol intake and caffeine, both of which can cause emotive thoughts; to work closely with your consultant in terms of medication; and, above all, to not dwell on thoughts. Let the intrusive thoughts go and move on to fresh, positive thinking. This advice is not easily given; I understand how challenging and difficult this can be. However, the only person who can cure you is yourself. It took me a long time to understand and accept this fact but it does work with grit and determination. Medication is there to support you on your journey but it is not the cure; only you can find that through strong thinking and, at the end of the day, common sense.

It is easier to give in to the intrusive thoughts than to walk away from them. I suspect that similar strengths are needed to fight any addiction. It's easy to neutralize the intrusive thought that slipped into your life after days of well-being. The fix seems simple and effective. I promise you that this is the route to disaster because, the next time, you will need to neutralize twice or more; you'll then begin the backward step into OCD. While it is easy to say the answer is to walk away, this action is tough and draining. The reward is a feeling of well-being that will come into your mind but this feeling is hard won. Believe in the guidance of professional help and work with the solutions. It can be one of the hardest times of your life but when you suddenly experience silence and become aware of your surroundings, the pain and challenge become justified. To listen to the birds singing or to simply undertake an act without repeating the action numerous times are exciting rewards.

You must remember that OCD is not a rare condition unique to you. There are many individuals out there who quietly suffer the same inhibitions that we all had as our condition began to impact on our lives. I have met a fellow sufferer within my wider family circle and I think it has done us good to talk about our experiences, although we are on different curves in terms of our recoveries. OCD is a terrible illness without help: recovery is about talking and challenging these awful feelings and thoughts. Thanks to many dedicated and supportive people, progress is being made to make this type of illness acceptable, understood and remedied.

My final thoughts are around the intangibility of OCD. Make no mistake in that OCD is a real disability but, as with any mental illness, most people are unable to either recognize or acknowledge the pain a sufferer is going through. While a physical disability is easily seen, OCD often adversely impacts on lives – both of the sufferer and their family and friends – in silence. Apart from the mental turmoil and stress, many sufferers lose many minutes or, worse, hours of each day, every day. Over a lifetime, years can be lost. I realize that without this disability it is possible that I may have been even more successful. However, OCD has taught me to be thoughtful and sensitive to facets of life and once you understand what is wrong with you there are many positives to come through from this experience. I guess all I am saying is to not look back, but forward. There is a way forward but it is up to each of us to grab our own feeling by the scruff of the neck, look it in the eye and determine how we manage ourselves to go onwards. It is difficult to concede but I do believe that I am a better person for what I have suffered, but I would not wish the experience on anyone!

And over two years on – how do I feel now? Well life is not always a bed of roses; there are, of course, good days and bad days. However, the point is there *are* good days and, in fact, great days! The main learning curve is the need to manage yourself. Understand the things that make *you* vulnerable to OCD and then manage them. For example, tiredness makes me more vulnerable to OCD so I try to manage my life to avoid being tired. Medication is also an issue; I should have had painkillers, not antidepressants, during the ongoing problems with my arm. You need to understand why thoughts intrude and this understanding can help to find the balance against OCD. So if you are having a bad day, sitting in recovery in hospital, it might just be a case of saying I am in pain and under medication, so perhaps there will be intrusive thoughts. Acceptance helps the dismissal.

To sum up my story, I still work in a responsible position and I am beginning to really enjoy life again. I look forward to events at long last. It has not been easy and I am very grateful to a very understanding wife and children. We never made a secret of my illness and have been very open and honest at home. For me improving OCD is about being honest with yourself that there is a real problem and talking to the right people – I would advocate talking rather than medication (including alcohol!) every time. As an OCD sufferer, you need to be understood and helped to help yourself. My worse setback was being treated for depression through standard medication. OCD is a bully and bullies need to be stood up to. There are good, helpful websites and specialist books available to help direct you and, thanks to a group of dedicated specialists, this awful disorder is being tackled. If you follow the guidance and be strong, I can assure you, it really does get better.

4

Handling the dragon

I'll take you back to 1963, I was just seven and everything was fine in our family until my three-year-old sister died of cancer. Mystery surrounded the illness and after being told of the death I remember thinking, 'I'll never have a happy head again.' In 1963 there was no bereavement counselling. My parents dealt with this by immersing themselves in their careers and I was left to my own imaginative devices, spending many of the following years feeling separated from my parents. Eventually my parents moved abroad with the Royal Air Force and, as my mother was unhappy with my schooling in rural Norfolk and I had failed my eleven-plus exams, I was sent to boarding school. I was left not only with an immense sense of loss, but somehow also with a great feeling of guilt.

During these early years I suffered many periods of unfounded anxiety, triggered by small events: a kiss from someone's granny when I was seven made me wonder whether I going to die from arthritis; seeing copulating dogs when I was nine made me a little aroused and I thought, 'Am I attracted to animals?' Anxiety led to a need for breathing exercises at boarding school when I was aged ten, by fourteen I was conducting checking rituals, and by sixteen I had a great fear of getting pregnant. Seeing a theatrical depiction of a Colditz prisoner going mad and performing rituals made me worry that I was going mad, too, which led to seeking reassurance from a psychiatrist at a clinic in Norfolk. He said, 'The only thing mad about you are your platform shoes!' I left reassured.

Following boarding school I only had brief periods with my parents, as I lived away from home in Norwich, then London and then Bristol, where I attended art school. Aged seventeen I feared I might be gay, and a couple of years later, while studying for an art degree, I developed a guilt about not being caring enough, or left-wing or political enough. The college psychiatrist pronounced I was locked in 'a parent and child thing'. I wasn't too sure what to make of that.

Despite intense ruminations and anxiety I managed to get a good degree and, aged twenty-two, moved to Amsterdam with my partner. There, lost in the loneliness of the day whilst my partner was away at work, I started to hyperventilate from time to time, which I attributed to drinking alcohol, and so gave up alcohol for two years – possibly the only benefit of OCD for me!

Returning to England at the age of twenty-five, I developed various rituals to control my weight, which at the time seemed to be the only thing I could control. We were living in a friend's half-built house, with no heating, and I was left alone to do the chores and cooking. Early each morning I'd swim forty-two lengths of the local Olympic-size swimming pool. For the walk there and back I adopted lucky pavement stones and marks on the ground, which I would have to touch or circle three times. During this period my weight plummeted below six stone and my monthly periods stopped.

In my case the OCD subject matter can take abstract forms – I have heard some call it 'pure O', that is pure obsessions, without the compulsions normally associated with the condition. Around about this time, listening to a news item about a serial killer, Dennis Nilsen, made me anxious about why people kill, and ponder whether could I become a killer? The worry started: 'Could I be a murderer?' and was accompanied by feelings of high anxiety. My mind spun, blocking the doors to logic and my thoughts quickly evolved quickly into 'I'm an artist, a visual person, and I'll never see inside a body unless I kill,' along with negative predictions that I'd always be a sad and worried person. During this period I tried various things to calm the anxiety, including applying for and being accepted on a medical illustration course. My parents suggested, in humorous desperation, writing to the then popular *Jim'll Fix It*, the television programme aimed at making people's wishes come true, to request that Jim find a body for me to look inside of . . .

However, the anxiety became intense, by far the most severe I had experienced up to that point, and I returned to live with my parents, labouring in a back room making obsessively detailed drawings. One evening, my mother excitedly called me to the television to watch a TV programme called *Your Life in Their Hands*. On this I watched a medical procedure, revealing some poor soul's internal, still living, organs, and somehow concluded that I didn't have to be a killer and went to bed feeling relieved. However, even before breakfast the next day I had come up with a new worrying thought, 'But I'll never see a brain, you can't see a brain without killing the owner.'

These thoughts intensified to the point where I sought help from a psychiatrist at the regional hospital and was subsequently admitted to their psychiatric clinic. It was there that I felt the most frightened I have ever felt in my life, and as with boarding school, I volunteered to go there, fearful of the unknown, yet hopeful. Not understanding the tricks that OCD can play, I compared myself to anorexics and self-harmers, whose pain I could understand, whose thoughts seemed more rational. I thought, 'Nobody here wants to see a brain, I must be really crazy, the worst case on the ward!'

I was treated the first week with the then preferred OCD medication and nobody explained the side effects – dry mouth, tremors, sensitive skin and increased anxiety. When this didn't do the trick I was given an additional 'calmer' drug, and within a couple of hours I was able to leave the ruminations behind and enjoy a bath, smelling the soap and feeling the warmth of the towels. Before this, even simple relaxation had been pushed from my life. The staff joked I'd had a 'miraculous recovery'. That evening I was even able to go out with my parents for an Indian meal and enjoy the outing. It was at this clinic I first encountered a psychologist who suggested various techniques to me. Being a Buddhist, his approach was enlightened, with some extra tricks that he felt were more effective than techniques such as thought-stopping, where I would ping a rubber band against my wrist whenever an intrusive thought occurred. He suggested concentrating on something I found beautiful, something that would in other times fill my senses, such as a field of new-mown hay, and he encouraged and praised my engagement in other activities, such as painting portraits of the other patients, having a manicure or just smiling. Although not a cure these eased slightly the momentum of my ruminations. Mindfulness and humour make a magic combo in any practitioner! He left me with the words, 'If it all happens again then just remember it's not important.' I left the clinic feeling fragile but free enough to participate in life, however with no real understanding or explanation as to what had happened to me. Up to this point the treatment I had received focused on dealing with the subject of my ruminations, rather than the mechanics.

It didn't take long for a subject of more importance than seeing a brain to pop up. I was still very fearful of having uncontrolled thoughts and terrible anxiety. After reading the biography of a person who entered into a decline because of 'unrequited love', I started to associate the symptoms with my own. When a male friend, for whom I had always held fond feelings, got engaged, I had the thought, 'What if he was the one? If my need for love is never satisfied I'll never recover, I'll never be happy.' This seemed a more tangible and real concern than the abstract thought of needing to see a brain. Losing myself in an illustration project I had been able to keep the ruminations and anxiety at bay.

I had a period of fifteen years, from my mid-twenties to late thirties, without drug treatment, during which time my mother died of a brain tumour and I had a number of disabling obsessions. The descent into ruminations and anxiety usually happened during times of stress, such as completing my college degree, feeling lonely in Amsterdam and when there were strains in my relationships.

From a very young age I had always had a talent for drawing, but low self-esteem and self-criticism hampered my dream of becoming an artist and illustrator, through fear of yet another bad patch. I like to draw with the radio or music on in the background, but when depressed or obsessed I'd work in silence. I would tell myself that I'd lost my spontaneity and couldn't draw as well as when I was happy, I wouldn't give myself a chance. There was a waterfall of negative predictive thoughts. My parents called it 'Jane's Phobias'.

I'd use my intellect to both seek and deny reassurance, and I'd build networks of 'supporters' to discuss the ruminations with. My ruminations were constantly evolving, always finding another interpretation, another loophole and another concern to be answered, driving my partner, father and various experts to, and sometimes beyond, the edge of exhaustion. Always, the ruminations were accompanied by varying degrees of anxiety, often unbearable, and made me incapable of working, of friendship, of doing the simplest of day-to-day tasks.

Over the years I sought help from my GPs, local mental health teams and private psychotherapists. I also used hard exercise as a form of self-help, running, swimming and cycling long distances; my running was so obsessive I was on target to run marathons in under three hours! If I lost count of how many lengths of a pool I had swum I would have to do extra lengths just to be on the safe side!

Looking back over the past thirty years it's interesting to note how both the diagnosis and the treatments have evolved. I have been prescribed all the usual OCD medications, as well as some others. The varying side effects ranged from dry mouth, low libido and weight gain to the more worrying dystonia, that is, involuntary muscle movements, and hyponatremia. The latter, a condition where the body chemistry goes haywire, put me in a coma for thirty-six hours!

After this frightening experience of hyponatremia I went back to psychotherapy. Because of my increased anxiety, which I feel was made worse by the medication, I contacted the psychologist that I'd worked with before, and respected, although he said he wouldn't take me on if I continued with the private psychotherapy. He again encouraged me to engage in various activities, so I made and decorated cakes for my loved ones, and partook in life drawing. I began to recover by doing things I enjoyed, but I was still plagued by a thought that my 'feelings' had been damaged beyond repair, causing depression, and that I would always be depressed (yet another catastrophic thought!). It was also the time the psychologist first mentioned 'obsession' to me. He told me my fear of damaged emotions was merely a horrible thought.

In addition to the help offered by the local NHS teams I had often consulted private 'talking' psychotherapists. These consultations often involved long discussions of my early childhood experiences and current relationships. Although these sessions provided some insight they never taught me how to deal with the condition in a meaningful way. In fact, these sessions may have fuelled my tendency to ruminate, and that was why my new psychologist wanted me to stop these sessions.

The psychotherapy techniques I've seen through the years have been many, trying to identify significant events in my past, simple behavioural therapy and thought-stopping, through to the most successful, for me, cognitive behaviour therapy. Occasionally I encountered treatment conflicts between the various people trying to help me. One psychiatrist wanted me to start taking lithium to control my anxiety, while a locum on the same team was quietly advising against this.

I always approached treatment with hope. Looking back, sometimes the contrast between treatments was vast. For example, during an initial outpatient appointment with a behavioural psychologist at the local mental health unit, I was bizarrely asked the opening question, 'When was it that I first masturbated?' – still very confusing to me! I found his approach baffling, so then bought my partner in to the sessions. The psychologist also wanted me to write down every time I was successful in not engaging with a ruminative thought. I completed his sheets with confusion, to keep him happy, and just continued on with my ruminations! I tried other distractions, such as taking a Biology O level.

Going back about ten years from today I started on a rollercoaster that encompassed changing medication, childbirth, followed by alcoholism and separation from my family! I found it hard to engage with my baby and much later it was suggested that I was suffering from post-natal depression. Eventually I managed to cease drinking, engaged in a detox programme and entered a rehab centre. Following this I stayed with my father and it was here that I was reunited with my son, lifting my feelings of depression.

At the age of about fifty, I eventually spent several months as an in-patient at a specialist anxiety unit. Here I was more positively treated as an individual and, importantly, the staff were very constructive and informative –

an improvement on the confusing atmospheres I had previously encountered. I was a resident along with a number of other OCD sufferers, which was a wonderful supportive change from the usual OCD isolation.

I was able to have my bicycle with me and each day continued to cycle, one of my thought-clearing and anti-anxiety activities; I had a little cycling mantra to get me going: 'Let it go . . . Be free . . . Now is now . . . Let me see!' I would concentrate on an active form of mindfulness, another technique I learned during this spell, which involved focusing on the things I cycled past, such as different coloured parked cars, trees, dog-walkers, motorists and a smiling schoolboy. I focused on what was really there, rather than the thing going round in my mind. The fact that cycling requires concentration, for safety's sake, helped focus my mind . . . bonuses all round: focus plus fitness!

At the specialist OCD unit, my history was looked at in an informative light; rather than focusing on the problematic past. In addition, the benefit of problem-solving was explained to me in order to help me find my core, inner beliefs and recognize those that were detrimental. The approach was much more hands on. I was coached to recognize thinking traps, and thinking errors, and to give myself permission to counter these with more balanced alternatives. I was trained not to be bossed around by OCD thoughts that cast personal shadows of depression. I learnt that I shouldn't try and swat the worrying wasp of OCD – it just comes back to sting again.

I was given the understanding that I was a serial 'what-if-er'. In my life my father encouraged me to draw both happy and sad things, so in my mind I like to imagine 'what if?' in the character of a dragon.

I discovered how to celebrate my mother's good features, but also recognize her low self-esteem, defensiveness and tendency of swiftness to anger. In her eyes I felt I was a failure, a bad egg, a view that I no longer hold. I recognized this as a central, negative, core belief. Shown the power of taking a risk and 'just doing', I realized I could be a reasonable mother, and nothing is just black and white, there is a balanced, more smudgy, way in between.

The therapists in this unit used diagrams to explore and illustrate ideas, which worked much better with my visual side. I discovered the OCD is just one instrument but it makes the whole orchestra play its tune.

As my confidence in my art work was still low I found it helpful to engage in what I call 'halfway house' activities, meaning not aiming for a masterpiece and having a go at something different, such as making and decorating a bowl in the pottery. The facilities for occupational therapy were very good, and there was a good deal of fun and discovery. Cherish the success in the moment.

Recovery

A key lesson I learnt involved the 'cognitive' of cognitive behaviour therapy. I was guided into understanding, facing and accepting the negative consequences of my condition, and to put some thought towards how the condition was holding back my engagement with the world. I started to ask myself the question: 'is it really worth it?' when my ruminations demanded my thoughts.

Now, three years after leaving the specialist OCD unit, I live at home with my son and husband, and I'm doing my share of the daily routines, including the enjoyable, chatty bus rides to and from school with my son. Daily routines of chores, exercise, work and school runs have replaced the electric anxiety of the past.

I've completely left behind any desire to return to alcohol, and with the techniques I learnt at the specialist OCD unit I feel capable of dealing with the ruminations that do pop up, and no longer feel a need to consult psychotherapists.

With my new self-belief I'm starting to produce, and sell, my artwork, and have even been offered a solo exhibition in a couple of years' time!

I am a non-perfect roly-poly middle-aged woman of fifty-three but I now feel like I'm an emotional millionaire! I felt I was at core a bad egg; I left the specialist OCD unit as an all-right egg, with ambitions for the future – more of a free range egg, more mentally flexible.

My son wrote recently on his birthday card to me, 'Not even a dinosaur could take me away from you'! I now say for certain that the dragon of OCD will not take me from him. The OCD dragon is capable of breathing its fire into any doubts, but now, no matter what the subject of my ruminations, each time recovery for me is about turning my interest to something I genuinely value in my life.

5

From the brink

Nearly nine years ago at the end of 2001, I was clinically diagnosed with OCD. This in turn brought on my first bout of serious depression.

After a number of appointments with an excellent psychiatrist he concluded that he was almost certain I was suffering from OCD and probably had been from the day I was born.

My first memory of this condition is from when I was age five, thirty-seven years ago. My mum had to tell me that Father Christmas didn't exist because I couldn't stop thinking about what would happen if some 'bad man' killed Father Christmas, took his place and then killed my family and me. So for about three years I was the only one at school that knew Father Christmas wasn't real. This was a pretty big thing for a five-year-old, especially when here was something that should have been lovely, with nothing bad connected to it at all, but my OCD had managed to invent something and then make it very real.

It was around this time that I started having to even things up. For instance, if I knocked my left arm, I had to knock my right arm, and if I scratched the right side of my chin, I had to do the same with the left side.

This then developed into 'number cancelling/evening', in which everything was multiplied, added, subtracted or divided by the number '6'. I chose '6' because it is part of 666, the number of the devil/the beast. I was scared of the unknown – it seemed possible to me that there was some kind of evil force out there, and I had no way of either proving or disproving its existence.

By the time I reached eleven, I had already endured years of a terrible relationship with my father; he was a cruel and petty man, and I was terribly scared of him. This relationship just fed my OCD and gave me numerous more fears, most notably a fear of prison. My dad would constantly tell me that I would end up in prison one day! (The irony of this was that I was a good kid, always wanting to please, with a generous nature.) My OCD was only too pleased to latch on to this and let my dad stir up an awful fear in me that took no notice of any reality I could summon up.

It is important to point out that, as well as all these different areas in which my OCD materialized, I would think constantly, non-stop, of worst-case scenarios, which were then mulled over for hours, days and weeks, trying to find a way to neutralize or even them out.

From the age of eleven to sixteen I only attended high school for six months out of the whole five years. The culprit? Yes, OCD! At the time everyone said I was lazy, a problem child, a bunker (truant) . . . the list went on and on. My parents had no idea what was wrong and, in my dad's case, didn't care. My worsening OCD then brought on a stammer in me that had been totally absent before. This gave my father even more ammunition to use against me, which in turn made my stammer, and of course my

OCD, even worse. I saw a number of social workers and child psychologists and all of them had their theories about me, but all without exception were a million miles away from what the real problem was.

So at age sixteen I left school, having not really gone. I missed out on so much of my formative years because of my OCD. I will leave it up to others to imagine what effect missing virtually all of high school can have on a young person. Obviously I had no qualifications and no prospects, so, perhaps unsurprisingly, I found myself in a dead-end job at sixteen. I also had all the usual worries and fears of any teenager – girls, self-esteem, acne, peer acceptance – but all made tenfold by OCD.

As I matured I gained more knowledge every day, as we all do, just living our lives. I also gained more worries due the fact that the more we know and understand, the more information there is to obsess and fret about. The only thing that kept me going for the next five years, from age sixteen to twenty-one, was my one real passion and talent: tennis! By the time I was twenty-one I was ranked in the top forty players in Great Britain – I really was a prospect. But guess what? By the time I was twenty-two my tennis game had been destroyed by my OCD. I obsessed constantly about my technique, which in turn developed into many doubts about all of my strokes and actually ruined my tennis, to the point where I could hardly hit a ball anymore. So I was left with no choice but to give up before I could really take advantage of my opportunity.

Looking back now, I realize that my OCD would get its teeth into anything I cared about. On the very rare occasions when I didn't have anything on my mind, my mind would scan my brain and look for things to obsess about.

I recall going to Spain for a week with friends and only leaving the villa on three occasions because of non-stop obsessing about so many different things, like the way I looked . . . was I too fat? . . . was I too white? . . . if I went out and met women and they didn't like me, would it really hurt my confidence and therefore take away my last remaining bit of self-belief? On another occasion, I drove for ninety minutes to the countryside, walked my dog for about two hours, then drove the ninety-minute trip home – I was hardly able to remember what I done for those five hours as I was so far inside my head. It was always the same story with anything I cared remotely about: my OCD would attack it.

My OCD really escalated as I got older: the more I knew in life, the more my OCD battled against me. My mood deteriorated and I had my first serious bout of depression; at age thirty-four I sought out and received my first diagnosis, medication and therapy from the aforementioned psychiatrist.

He prescribed me an antidepressant for my depression and found me a good psychologist who specialized in cognitive behaviour therapy (CBT) and who started helping me with my OCD. This therapy helped a fair amount but not enough! In hindsight if anyone has OCD you need to seek a therapist or psychologist who *specializes* in OCD. Remember, standard CBT is the right therapy for depression, but it's the opposite of what's right for your OCD, the reason being is that *standard* CBT teaches you to *challenge* thoughts, whereas specialized OCD therapy teaches you to sit with and embrace your fears and worries. All I wanted was to get well again and I was prepared to do anything I was told to do to get better. But now I know that I needed to really embrace, understand and live the experiences of my depression and severe OCD, and of course have an OCD specialist! If you don't learn about your OCD and depression, they are very likely to come back and, next time, they are likely to be stronger.

From being in a bad place I managed to improve my mental health in about eighteen months but, as I was to find out in the future, all I had done was to push the OCD and depression to one side for now.

For the next couple of years after this, I returned to my previous state of living with my OCD and depression – I had lots of worries but not quite enough to push me over the edge.

I would like to point out here that depression will generally follow severe OCD, because one way a depression can develop is from a constant flow of negativity in your head, which in turn can push you into a depression.

By the time I had turned thirty-seven my OCD had a reached a level that was so bad that I felt I had lost my mind! I was trapped inside my brain with my negative thoughts and fears. I wasn't sleeping or eating and had started drinking a lot to numb my brain. In no time I had fallen into a very deep depression. On a scale of 1 to 10 (with 10 being the most severe), if last time was a 5, this time it was a 9!

I returned to my original psychiatrist who excelled as he had before, mainly due to the fact that he totally understood me. He was someone I connected with and was a master of his craft, but it still wasn't enough to keep me out of hospital for my depression. We hadn't even started to deal with the OCD yet as the depression had to be tackled first, and the therapies for OCD and depression can contradict one another.

It was while I was in hospital that my psychiatrist got my medication right: one medication for my OCD and a different one for my depression. These tablets continue to give me the support and strength that is needed to tackle these two illnesses. I continued with my CBT for depression and was making daily progress, but I was at a loss to find someone who really understood my OCD 100 per cent. I felt that finding the right specialist was the key to my recovery, and they would help me to understand and live with my OCD. Remarkably there wasn't an OCD specialist at one of the top hospitals in the UK; the available therapists were standard CBT therapists, so I had to search for an OCD expert myself. When you're seriously ill, this is the last thing you have strength for.

I found a couple of specialists over the next six months but, to be honest, neither of them was very good! I thought that they didn't understand and feel OCD. As I was to find out, anyone who suffers from OCD needs to have a therapist that feels it inside and out, and is not just passing on information from a text book.

After these two very disappointing experiences, I was in a bookshop one Saturday morning looking for a book that could help me in some way. I came across one written by two OCD specialists and ended up reading it from cover to cover that weekend. I felt the authors had written the book for me – I felt for the very first time that someone could really understand what I was going through. On the following Monday I managed to get in contact with one of the authors and I had a ten-minute telephone conversation with him; I really felt this was someone who would help me.

Over the next twelve months I saw the author, who was a cognitive behaviour therapist, and he helped me to understand OCD. He did this by passing on to me his knowledge of my condition – it's like he knew exactly how I felt and what I was thinking. I started to understand my own OCD and see it for what it was, which is a very clever and manipulating condition that preys on the weaknesses of any human being who develops any symptoms. I followed all his advice: this included living a healthy lifestyle, keeping physically fit, no alcohol and frequent exposure to my fears. These were mainly that I had done something illegal, and that the police would be investigating me for all sorts of crimes that my OCD had told me I may have committed. As part of my treatment, I had to read headlines in the newspapers and online about people who had been arrested or convicted. I would also drive to a huge prison on a daily basis and would sit outside for twenty minutes imagining that I may have to go inside for a crime. When I started this my stress level was so very high – I would constantly negate my fears by telling myself that I would never have to go inside a prison but, of course, all this did was keep my stress levels up. Eventually I would sit with my fears and anxieties and not try to neutralize them. After a period of time my stress levels were barely detectable; I could sit outside any prison or see any police car and not have even a flicker of fear or anxiety.

One of the things I realized was that any form of OCD is terrible but I feel that it is even more so if it is a mental ritual as opposed to a physical ritual – this is not to say that a physical ritual isn't bad, but with a physical one at least you're able to have something you can try to stop doing. With a mental ritual, most of the time you don't realize you're doing it and your brain is just running riot.

Another thing my therapist made me realize was that if I had two good days and then one bad day, that was all right, because bad days are part of the process of getting better!

And then one day it all seemed to become much clearer to me.

For the previous thirty-nine years I had been trying to neutralize all these scary, fearful and anxious thoughts by trying to find calming solutions to them. I did this by constant analysing in my head and seeking reassurances from any outside source available, but all I succeeded in doing was to just keep feeding them.

The clarity came for me when my perspective totally shifted and I realized it wasn't about eliminating the thoughts that give you fears, worries and anxieties from your everyday living, as this would be impossible for any human being to do! It is about not *interacting* with those obsessive thoughts. The more I tried to neutralize my thoughts and put myself at ease, the worse and more intense they became. Even when I have the worst and most obtrusive thoughts, fears and visions in my head (and as far as I am concerned they are 100 per cent real), I just have to sit with them and not neutralize them, and then my anxiety level will eventually drop to 0 per cent. As a result I can live my life normally, and the fears have zero impact. It's hard to put into words, but it means not trying to eliminate your bad thoughts through seeking reassurance, not trying to get 'that even feeling', but trying your damn hardest to completely change your perspective on the way your thought patterns works. It's about just sitting with your thoughts until your anxiety and stress levels drop to an unnoticeable level and you can live your life normally.

So I managed to summon every last bit of courage and strength I had. I started to discover that ever so slightly my anxiety and stress started to decrease. I continued to battle away over the first few days, which then became weeks and months. I found, bit by bit, that I was getting better. This gave me the encouragement I needed to continue fighting my OCD.

After about eight or nine months I started to really get some clarity. I think the reason this started to happen was due to all the courage and strength I was showing and also my genuine willingness to change my perspective in the way I thought about my fears and worries. After much effort, and with my therapist insisting I live with the experience and learn and understand about OCD and depression, I got to the point where I was much better.

I now know how to live with my OCD and keep it at bay virtually all the time but, believe me, it is always trying to find a way in, so I need to always be on my guard every day.

I know my OCD will always be hanging around in the background but I now know I can and do live with it. I have the knowledge, and most importantly the perspective, to live a happy life!

OCD dominated and, at one stage, virtually destroyed my life, but there is an incredible silver lining to my story.

I feel that living the OCD experience has given me vast amounts of wisdom, knowledge and a perspective that allows me to look at life with an open mind. I'm able to see things objectively and have lost many of the insecurities that I had previously, like worrying what people think about me, fears about what may go wrong in the future and the normal day-to-day worries, stresses and fears that everyone has. I have a lot more compassion towards others and myself now and am able to live 'in the moment' most of the time.

From the brink of looking up at the sky at God knows what, wondering if there is any point to life, and in so much pain with OCD and depression that I couldn't see myself ever getting better, I've reached a point where I'm healthy, happy and have the most wonderful partner anyone could ever wish for. I'm also lucky to run a successful business, have a huge passion for my dogs and cats, and my partner and I are looking forward to starting a family in the future.

So, there is hope for anyone who has severe OCD or depression or even both, but it is a courageous battle you need to fight. You certainly need an excellent therapist or psychologist and very possibly the right medication. But with the right support and help it's a battle you can most certainly win!

6

As common as a cold

If you have my form of OCD, you will have no doubt realized that most OCD literature is not really written for you. Sufferers who have obsessive hand-washing, checking or who hoard are all well covered in the literature but I think I can count on one hand the number of accounts I have read of people who have suffered from my kind of disturbing intrusive thoughts. This is despite the fact that I am told it is an extremely common form of OCD. I have agreed to write this story because I think that it is time that this balance was restored. Intrusive thoughts might be less obvious that other forms of OCD but I can vouch from my own experience and those of others I have met that they can be hugely destructive. When my OCD was at its worst I would have loved to have read an account from a fellow sufferer that was relevant to my intrusive thoughts and experiences. I hope this story can help at least one person out there . . .

Beginnings

I was diagnosed with OCD when I was twenty-two. I can't recall exactly when it started but I know that I was at primary school when I first became aware of the fact that I had the ability to think of horrendous things and that these thoughts would not go away however hard I tried. I must have been eight or nine years old at the time. So it took around thirteen to fourteen years for me to find out that there was a name for what I had and that other people had it! Looking back on this now it fills me with sadness and indeed anger that I had to endure this suffering in silence for such a huge length of time.

My first memory of being disturbed by intrusive thoughts was when I was walking down my street to my school and I suddenly had the thought that I was going to kill my mother. At the time the idea was probably the worst possible thought that I could think of. I was a total mummy's boy (I still am, I suppose – I didn't murder her by the way!); she meant everything to me. The thought that I could do anything to hurt my precious mum was one that I could not cope with: surely the thought meant I secretly wanted to do it? Were thoughts not almost as bad as deeds? Who could I talk to about this? What did the physical sensations mean that I experienced when I had the thought? (These were hot flushes, a constricted throat and a tingling sensation as the hair stood up on my body.)

I did not have the answers for any of these questions and because of this I could not dismiss the thoughts. I remember crying quite a bit at the time but only telling my parents that I had 'voices in my head'. I insisted on my dad walking to school with me, he knew that there was something wrong but I couldn't tell him what I was thinking; he would disown me! So my solution (a slightly strange one, I must admit) was to write down somewhere that I was not going to kill my mum. I chose a small bit of paper and wrote on it 'I will not kill my mum', put it in a book that I was confident that she would not read, and returned it to her bookshelf. I'm not sure what the logic was, but I suppose I thought that a physical expression could somehow beat my thoughts. Needless to say, it did not particularly work and it in fact it just became a symbol of how wicked I was, a fact that I was reminded of every time I walked past that room.

I associate this thought with being the beginning of my OCD because it had a numbers of aspects which really were to become the hallmarks of my illness: I could very easily think up things (which I now know are termed 'intrusive thoughts') which I could not control or cope with and which might torment me relentlessly; I would create symbols around me (like the book on my mum's bookshelf) which I could not escape and which served to support these thoughts and ensure that they persisted; and the thoughts resulted in physical sensations such as a constricted throat which, given the timing of when they occurred, seemed to present further proof that there must be something true about the thoughts. Why else would my hairs stand on end? Surely I must be excited by the idea of killing my mum?

The combination of these factors was a powerful cocktail and one that was to wreak inner havoc in my childhood and teenage years.

The early years

After a time the impact of the 'I am going to kill my mum' thought started to wane. It was not that the subject was any less upsetting but I think I may have got bored with it and realized that I could think of other upsetting thoughts to suit my particular preoccupations at the time.

The next thought I can recall was that I was going to be a tramp when I grew up. We lived about half a mile or so from a homeless shelter, outside which old men would stand or lie around in their filthy clothes, blind drunk on cheap lager. I told myself that I was going to end up like these men. It seems pretty comical now, but then it was dreadfully upsetting and whatever I tried I could not stop thinking of the thought. I hated it when we drove past the place, I would shut my eyes and hold my breath, only breathing out when we had cleared the area – a bit difficult if there was a traffic jam! I also remember even going to the lengths of putting a box over my head as we drove past once so I did not have to see the men. I can't remember for certain if I told my parents about this thought at the time but I think I did and they told me that 'everybody has thoughts like this'. I refused to believe it; I thought nobody can have thoughts as bad as this.

I can't recall if the 'tramp thought' happened before or after my sister was abused by one of the men from the shelter. I remember my dad coming to my school and taking me out for the afternoon. I was taken to a family friend's house who explained to me what had happened. I didn't really understand it but I remember how upset everybody was and thinking that the men at the shelter were disgusting. I also remember beating myself up because whilst we were meant to be looking after my sister, I continued to have intrusive thoughts about other things (perhaps about killing my mum but I can't recall). I felt that I must be really bad to not be able to devote myself 100 per cent to looking after my sister and to be distracted by other thoughts.

Teenage years

Once I discovered the destructive power I had over myself I think I also realized that I needed a coping mechanism to get me through this. I think this is the reason why I became so driven academically. The incessant barrage of intrusive thoughts meant that I had an extremely low opinion of myself; a way to somehow counteract this was to achieve externally verifiable success. Looking back on it now I was ridiculously focused on my marks in exams and essays from as early as the age of ten. I probably should have been outside kicking a ball around; instead, I was preoccupied with submitting the perfect pieces of work and receiving the most praise possible from my teachers. However, the problem was that I set the rules of the game against myself: if I did receive the 'A' grade I craved, I would glow with satisfaction for a few hours or perhaps days but if I failed to succeed, as I did once in a memorable (but actually not very important) exam, then it would be an absolute catastrophe that would have ramifications for weeks or months later. I was hugely sensitive to any possibility that I might fail at something; classmates would wind me up by telling me that we were having a test on that day that I had not revised for; I would pester my teachers for them to mark my essays quicker (I must have been so annoying!). My favourite teacher once said in my end of year report that I was 'outstanding' but 'too sensitive' and that I 'worried too much'. He was right. I was developing into a young man who had very little reserves of inner confidence or calm but one who was driven by external approbation with a perfectionist approach to everything he did. Not a great combination!

My teenage years therefore became about achieving a series of academic goals – end of year exams, GSCE mocks, GCSEs, A-level mocks, A levels, university entrance exams, etc. Achieving these goals did nothing to help the level of my intrusive thoughts, which continued to act as a veil over my happiness. Once one target had been achieved, its importance would disappear and I would move on to the next thing. Clearly I would run out of track at some point.

During this period the subject of my intrusive thoughts settled down and from then on they largely became variations on one or two single themes. I no longer worried about homelessness or even matricide but my intrusive thoughts were almost entirely focused on the fact that I was or would be gay. This was my most persistent intrusive thought and one that continued into adulthood. In any situation, a male person would become the subject of these intrusive thoughts: a teacher, a school friend or a family member. Given that around 50 per cent of the population are men it was always easy to find a target! The most upsetting one was the thought that I was somehow attracted to my dad; this was surely the height of depravity! Again my mind was filled with questions: Surely these thoughts must mean that I was more likely to do something about this? What would these people think if they knew what I was thinking? The thoughts were still accompanied by physical sensations, namely that my throat would become constricted, I would feel excess saliva in my mouth or the hairs on my legs would stand up. I would scan my body for any physical manifestations; did I just feel something in my crotch when I looked at that man? The more I tried to not have any physical sensations the more that I would; I told myself that these reactions were proof positive that I was gay. I now know that 'the body scan', as it is known, and the subsequent physical manifestations are very common with people with my form of OCD. The body scan is a powerful thing. Try it for yourself: close your eyes and concentrate your mind on your big toe. Do you feel it tingling or any other sensation there? If you do then you have just demonstrated the power of the mind over the physical. If you don't, well, good for you!

I also developed symbols that strengthened the power of the thoughts, for example the man's crotch and/or neck would become a symbol and I would think that if I was drawn to look at it, it must be proof of the fact that I was attracted to that person; it is pretty difficult to not look at something if you tell yourself that you shouldn't. At the same time I knew that avoidance was not the answer so I also subjected myself to basic exposure techniques – i.e. I would deliberately look at the man/boy's crotch or neck in the thought that if I looked at it for long enough I would be able to prove to myself that I was *not* somehow attracted. I don't think that I was ever successful in doing this because the physical sensations I experienced would increase my anxiety levels to an unbearable level. I would then engage in a tussle, on the one hand knowing that avoidance was not the answer, and on the other also knowing that it was the only thing I wanted to do so that I could escape this uncomfortable situation. Looking back I think this rudimentary exposure technique, whilst it was by no means ever completely successful, was actually pretty helpful; I did not see avoidance as an answer. I think I always felt at the time that, given the adaptability of my intrusive thoughts, to embrace avoidance would be an absolute disaster in my case. I think this realization has always prevented my OCD from degenerating.

What made this particular intrusive thought even more potent, I think, was that during my early teenage years I did have some homosexual experiences. I now know that this is pretty common for boys when they are going through puberty. However, at the time I saw these experiences as being a heinous crime that somehow proved that my intrusive thoughts were correct and that I might act on thoughts about my dad, teachers, friends or whoever at any given point. I tormented myself relentlessly about these experiences for well over five years and I can truly say that as a result I did not experience true happiness at any point during that time. My relationships with the friends with whom I had 'fumbled' disintegrated; I don't know whether this was because I wanted this to happen or because this is what happens to some friendships at that age – I will never know.

The experience was undoubtedly pretty influential in the development of the strength of my OCD. The logic I used was that for the first time there was a direct factual link between the subject of my OCD and reality; that is, hitherto I had not killed my mother or started to drink Tennants Super but in this case I had done exactly what my intrusive thoughts were about. I think this link to 'reality' meant that this particular intrusive thought was very powerful and persistent. I think it also put wind into the sails of my OCD in general because in my eyes it supported the view that the thoughts could have physical results. This was a dangerous development and I think greatly assisted in the progression of future illness.

The amount of time that I spent worrying about being gay now seems bizarre but it was my number one concern for years. Every man would be the target of my intrusive thoughts – handsome/ugly, old/young, fat/thin – I think I thought I 'fancied' them all at some point. The thoughts were amazingly easy to conjure up and always had the same predictable effects. The thoughts were very one-dimensional, which was a key aspect of their persistence since it enabled them to be activated quickly and 'on demand'. I never fantasized about men, but instead a flash of a man's face or just the thought of a friend at the wrong time was disaster. The most highly charged example of this was when I was masturbating (a common occurrence during those years!). As I masturbated I would fantasize about the long-awaited contact with girls and just as I was about to ejaculate the thought of a man or friend of mine would flash into my head. How could I have that thought at such a point? I could not mentally process it – it was simply unacceptable. Afterwards I would often cry myself to sleep. Waking in the morning I would have a short, blissful moment of forgetfulness before the memory of the night before came crashing in. It would stay with me for hours if not days afterwards.

Like most teenage boys I was desperate to start having sex with girls; for me though it had an added level of importance because I thought to myself that any demonstration of heterosexual prowess would eliminate my intrusive thoughts of being gay. There was a lot riding on my first girlfriends! From about sixteen I started sleeping with girls; the sex was great but it quickly became clear to me that this would not 'cure' me of my intrusive thoughts. If anything the fact that I was in such a highly charged and symbolic situation meant that if I had intrusive thoughts about a man at the wrong moment I would be even more disturbed. It was not just me anymore: what would the girl think of me if she knew that at the point of my ejaculation I'd had a thought about a friend of mine, my dad or even her dad? It was completely unacceptable and I tried desperately hard to suppress the thoughts. It is very hard to not think of something – just ask any psychologist about the pink elephant!

Early adulthood

By the time I was taking my A levels I'd had OCD for about ten years. The subject of my intrusive thoughts had stabilized; they were predictable and routine but they were agile and had lost none of their impact. I had a girlfriend but my intrusive thoughts made me feel like I was living a lie. I continued to throw myself into academic achievement – I was desperate not to fall behind as I was not sure what my life meant without this spurring me on. At the back of my head was the thought that maybe if I got to university there was always the chance that I might outgrow my intrusive thoughts.

This was around the time that a new intrusive thought came my way. This time it was that I am or am going to become a paedophile. Maybe I was getting a little bit bored of the intrusive thoughts about me being gay and my OCD decided to give me some variety. It took very much the same form as the other intrusive thought but was more upsetting. Visions of children I knew would come into my head when I least wanted them. I would deliberately look at children to ensure that I could prove to myself that I was not a paedophile. However my tolerance for the anxiety that this caused was less because the implication of this intrusive thoughts being true was horrific in the extreme. The anxiety was intense, the hair on my legs would stand up, I would feel a lump in my throat and I would produce extra saliva, all of which I interpreted as some kind of proof of some kind of arousal.

The intrusive thoughts on the two subjects would interchange throughout the day. The paedophile thoughts packed the biggest punch but the thought of being gay continued to get a reaction. It is certainly a strange combination of thoughts to come up with and I would like to make clear to the reader that I have always thought it was really unfair on gay people how I could juxtapose the two things. I suppose in a way the subject matter was irrelevant: it was the fact that they were both things that I was worried about and my mind and body just decided to react to them in the same manner.

University was 80 per cent great. I met my best friends there, I had a string of girlfriends, I partied hard and I became a lot more socially confident. Interestingly, studying became less important to me; I did enough to get the grade I wanted but not much more. I think that I realized that I did not want to become a career academic and I consciously decided to maximize the social experience. This was, of course, a healthy departure from my previous overly academically driven frame of mind. The bad 20 per cent was dominated by my OCD and at times I must confess that it felt like much more than 20 per cent. A small part of me expected it all to go away but this was not to be and my intrusive thoughts actually gained an additional poignancy because it felt like I was polluting a good experience and good people. My mind would be infiltrated at the wrong points during sex; and I would work myself up to an anxious state around my newfound friends as I told myself that I was in danger of touching them inappropriately.

One particularly vivid memory is of me sitting in the toilet of a pub toilet curled up in a ball and crying because I could not get out of my head a picture my best friend's baby brother which he had on his wall. The picture became a symbol of my supposed paedophilia – why else would such a inconsequential thing make me so anxious? Again, the intrusive thought was just a superficial thought of his face or even just an idea but it made me wracked with guilt. I felt that I was intruding on and perhaps even contaminating my friend's life by having these thoughts; that he would disown me if he knew; and that I really didn't deserve friends like this. I had no strategy to deal with this and this meant that a streak of profound unhappiness continued through my otherwise great experience at university.

My love life also become progressively more complex as time went on, and I ended up particularly hurting one girlfriend who didn't deserve to be hurt. I don't know whether this had anything to do with the OCD but it certainly did not help my ability to maintain relationships at the time.

University didn't cure me of the 'thoughts in my head'. As my time at university drew to a close I think I also realized that I couldn't go on forever chasing after some external validation of attainment to avoid facing up to my illness. Something had to give.

The catalyst for change

I didn't have to wait long to run out of track. After university I moved back home to live with my parents and began a prestigious postgraduate course. My fellow students were all brilliant and amazingly driven but I was not sure what I was doing there. At the same time my complicated university love-life unravelled and I was single just at the time when my social life took a dive. Many of my best friends were away travelling so I became more reclusive, and I suppose living at home didn't help either. The work mounted up and my self-recrimination about my disastrous love-life also built. What really tipped me over the edge to a fully fledged breakdown, though, was just the realization that I could not go on like this: my intrusive thoughts were still ever present and without any more external validations of success or stepping stones to a new life I would need to at last deal with my problems. I got off the train.

I dropped out of my postgraduate course. It happened over a period of a couple of weeks: I missed the first essay deadline and then just stopped going in. At first I did not really fully accept that I had dropped out because the implication of giving up on academic achievement and falling behind my peers was unprecedented and scary. I stayed in bed for about six weeks. I was like a hermit: I didn't take calls or go out. My mum and dad were terribly worried about me and often took the day off work to ensure that I ate and drank properly. My intrusive thoughts continued unabated but they were now joined by a dangerous ally: depression. The depression gave me a deep sinking feeling. The only place that I wanted to be was alone and in bed. At one point I thought that if I didn't eat anymore it would eventually resolve the problem of my intrusive thoughts for me. I think I lasted about three days or so and as a result I became physically weak and as thin as a rake.

Part of me was relieved, though. I had stopped my relentless focus on attainment and the future, and instead I could focus on what was wrong with me. This sense of relief became stronger and eventually I agreed to go to the doctor to discuss my problems. I also started going to the gym, bought a bike and even got a job in a local restaurant as a waiter.

The beginnings of treatment

I can't really blame the GP for not diagnosing my OCD. I had never discussed properly the content of my intrusive thoughts – I was ashamed and I was not going to do so to someone I didn't know. What would happen if I told her the thoughts about me being a paedophile? Would she see me as risk to children and call up the police? I skirted around the subject and talked mostly about my depression and just about the thoughts going on in my head. She prescribed me an SSRI antidepressant and recommended that I started therapy. She didn't recommend any particular form of therapy and unfortunately I did not ask as I didn't know any better. She did say one memorable thing that has always stuck with me, though: that mental illness is very common in people in their twenties (and, interestingly, particularly prevalent in men) and that in her experience by the time many people are into their thirties they often begin to recover because they just cannot be bothered with the mental effort of being ill anymore. I think I know what she meant now, though at the time I was just pleased that there was hope . . .

The doctor warned me that the antidepressant would not work immediately. From memory I think she said that it took about five weeks to work and that I could feel worse before I felt better. I was ambivalent about taking medication: on the one hand I wanted to feel better and for it to take some of the pain away, but on the other I felt a stigma associated with being on medication and did not want to become dependent on it. I started taking the drug and did indeed feel worse. I also started to develop physical symptoms including ejaculation becoming really difficult to achieve. I also have to admit that, like many people with mental illness, I was not particularly good at taking the medication. I would miss out days and forget to order repeat prescriptions until it was too late, and I would sometimes drink too much when out with friends. Now knowing a little more about how these drugs work I realize what a stupid approach I took to taking the medication; for them to be effective one needs to be disciplined about taking them regularly and consistently – doing it my way just made the whole thing much harder on myself. I don't think that I ever really gave the antidepressant I was on a real chance to work.

My doctor did not provide any assistance in setting up a course of therapy. In the end I had to find my own therapist through my parents' connections. It turned out the guy I ended up seeing was a psychoanalytic therapist. I was later told by a psychologist who specialized in the treatment of OCD that in his opinion this form of therapy is at best ineffective in the treatment of OCD and at worst can actually have a negative impact because it encourages OCD sufferers to ruminate and over analyse their thoughts. Writing now I can say that I completely agree with him, but at the time I had no knowledge of different therapies and so had to find this out for myself. The psychoanalytic therapist and I didn't really click, and after a couple of months we came to a mutual agreement to stop the sessions; rather than suggesting another form of therapy he presumed that our lack of progress was just an issue of personalities, and so he referred me to an association of psychoanalytic therapists (better to keep it in the family I suppose!). I turned up at the clinic and was given an hour's assessment with a well meaning but slightly irritating therapist. She was like a cliché – her face said 'I understand', she expressed no opinions herself, threw everything back on me and spent quite a long time asking strange questions about my childhood. However, it was the look of pity on her face and the constant pauses and the encouraging 'ah-ha' that got under my skin. Luckily for me, in the end she recommended another analyst closer to my home. I felt I'd had a narrow escape!

I saw my psychoanalytic therapist for the best part of two years; I probably also paid her thousands of pounds in fees. To be fair to her she did achieve what nobody had achieved before, which was to get me to talk openly about the nature of my intrusive thoughts. I trusted her and over a period of three to four months I was able to tell her everything. This was certainly a big breakthrough but, beyond that, we didn't really make much progress. She did not suggest that I might have OCD, nor did she particularly change her treatment later on when I told her that I had found out from a different source that I did have this form of mental illness. OCD is a well-armed fighting force and I found her techniques toothless in comparison; you cannot talk your way out of suffering from OCD! I enjoyed seeing her, though – we clicked, we talked a great deal and, if I am honest, I think I had a bit of a crush on her too! Nevertheless, I coasted along for months on end and I didn't learn any robust coping strategies to deal with the onslaught of my OCD. Unfortunately I also became dependent on her. She once told me that my face would visibly sadden if she had to cancel or announced that she was going on holiday. In fact, I did have some of my lowest points when she was unavailable.

I was very volatile during this period. I would fall to the depths of despair, including sitting crying for hours in the rain outside my parent's house, and I also ruminated about suicide. I even once drove 100 miles with some vague thoughts of throwing myself off a favourite cliff-top. I would also have some real highs as I made plans for the future: I was going to do a ski season; I was going to travel around South America; I would apply for another great postgraduate course somewhere. My parents and I discussed my treatment and, although I continued to see my psychoanalytic therapist, we agreed that I couldn't rely on her alone. I am in the lucky position of having educated middle-class parents who, if not necessarily well versed in all of the detail of mental health treatments, know people who are. A family friend suggested to my mum that it was time to see a psychiatrist. She gave us a recommendation and we booked at an appointment.

Diagnosis

I was pretty anxious about going to see the psychiatrist. What was I going to say to him? I couldn't rule out that he might say that I was a schizophrenic – didn't that mean that you had bad voices and thoughts in your head? Perhaps there was even a chance that I might be sectioned there and then. In the end seeing the psychiatrist was a godsend: he diagnosed me with OCD in ten minutes! I think once he knew that I didn't hear actual voices and that I realized (at least theoretically) that there was a difference between thoughts and reality that he became clear that it was OCD. He told me that the only treatment I should consider was a course of cognitive behaviour therapy (CBT); he recommended a specialist, and pre-scribed a new medication, a tricyclic antidepressant. He also said that what I had was treatable. I was elated.

Unfortunately it was not all plain sailing from there. I started on the new medication, which I was told was an older drug (it had been used much more widely before the invention of SSRIs) and had some side effects. The side effects were pretty distressing to be honest and, as well as interfering with sexual function, the drug also made me sweat profusely and gave me constipation. This was probably not helped by my continued lack of discipline in terms of taking the pills and my at times excessive con-sumption of alcohol. The other thing which didn't quite work out was that the CBT therapist who had been recommended lived over an hour away from my home so I decided (probably mistakenly) that I needed to find someone nearer to where I lived. My parents contacted the national society of psychologists that had been recommended by the psychiatrist, and the organization put us in touch with a clinical psychologist, apparently a specialist in CBT, who lived in our area.

He was nice enough. However, I'm not sure how much experience he truly had of the use of CBT in the treatment of OCD specifically. He was more of a general psychologist; he was also unfortunately a bit of a technocrat. He asked me to complete a number of questionnaires – one of them had over 500 questions about all aspects of my life including questions about my thoughts, sex life, etc! The questions were repeated throughout the questionnaire but in slightly different forms and I had to answer on a Likert scale, in other words, I had to choose from 'I totally agree' through 'I don't care' to 'I totally disagree'. Once I had completed the Herculean task of completing the survey he sent it somewhere and we waited for the results. At the next session he read out the findings to me. The main thing that I remember from this was that it said that I was 'confused about my sexuality'. Given the nature of my intrusive thoughts this, of course, was 'grist to the mill'. However, a part of me also realized that his survey was frankly complete rubbish. The survey did not distinguish between intrusive thoughts and other anxieties but I answered in the light of my specific problems; it then used its simplistic logic and spat out something that had all of the subtlety of pop psychology. The survey findings were also littered with other ridiculous findings: I had an addictive personality (because I confessed that I sometimes drank too much!), and I had an aggressive personality (because I had had a few fights in my lifetime!). Unfortunately, once again I had put my trust in somebody who professed to be an expert and I was let down. Many years later I told this story to my OCD specialist psychologist who said that this type of simplistic and lazy reasoning by mainstream psychologists is very common and is a big problem for the effective treatment of OCD in the population.

Confiding in people

I think that it was around this time that I told my family everything. I was nervous about doing this because of the morally reprehensible nature of some of my intrusive thoughts and also because some of them had featured my parents. I was not met with rejection or disapproval but instead they were just upset that I had subjected myself to such needless torture for such a long time. When I described the nature of my intrusive thoughts, they were not shocked by the content and said that they too in fact had similar thoughts often. The difference between them and me was that they were able to dismiss these thoughts quickly; it was only my ability to not let go of the thoughts which they could not understand. Confiding in my family was an essential step in my stabilization and later recovery – it is not a solution by itself (OCD is too strong for that), but it helps to de-stigmatize the thoughts and having at least one trustworthy person to confide in also helps to prevent you falling into depression when your OCD just becomes too much.

Work

Just under a year after my breakdown I decided that I should get a full-time job. I got a temporary job which was later made permanent; it was in a sector that I had never really thought about before but one that I found out that I actually really enjoyed. The discipline of work was really good for me, the social interaction which it requires and the focus on external tasks was like a breath of fresh air given my time spent at home festering alone with my intrusive thoughts; in fact, I would go as far as to say that it was actually easier going to work than staying home with myself! The intrusive thoughts were still bad and I still did not have any viable strategy of dealing with them. The symbols I created around me and the physical sensations still acted to reinforce my thoughts. I was also still pretty volatile – I would wake up most mornings with a deep sinking feeling and it felt like at any moment I could easily slide back into a breakdown. Nevertheless I persevered and hauled myself out of bed each morning. By the time my workday got to around 10 or 11 a.m. my personal problems would start to feel slightly less of an issue and I would experience small stretches of time, when I was concentrating on a particular task, where the thoughts would not bother me at all. I have worked ever since and I think it has been critical in the containment of my OCD.

During this time I continued to get treatment once a week in the evening from my psychoanalytic therapist and I think around once per month from the clinical psychologist. Psychologists will tend not to work outside normal work hours so I have always needed to thread my appointments around work commitments. This is certainly doable and my work has always been reasonable about me going to the 'doctors' provided that I have given them notice.

At around the same time I fell in love. It was a whirlwind romance and it became very serious very fast. I was pretty anxious at the same time for, whilst I really wanted to be in this relationship, I was also in a vulnerable state and it felt somehow that I was handing over the control of my destiny to somebody else. She was great to be around but something about her made me insecure. She was supremely independent; she had her own friends whom she kept at a distance; she was ambitious and it always felt somehow that she had another agenda which ultimately didn't involve me.

A personal setback

The relationship lasted about a year and when it ended it was a disaster (as I always felt it was going to be). My heart had not just been broken it had been decimated. I would check my answerphone every day for calls from her, I would try in vain to reignite the relationship by sending gifts or emailing her, and I would worry friends and family by idolizing her and trying to find ways to get back with her again. During this period my intrusive thoughts about being gay or a paedophile of course continued as ever. Added to this I heaped on recriminations about my conduct during the relationship. I also convinced myself that I was doomed to being single and my best friends all starting to settle down around me really nailed down the coffin lid!

I was not living with my parents anymore and had bought an apartment where I lived with a good friend. I had also moved to a new company which had turned out to be somewhat of a disappointment. From time to time I saw the general psychologist and continued seeing my psychoanalytic therapist on a weekly basis (it was an expensive business!). The latter announced during that time that she was moving and that I could no longer be her patient; when she said it I took it in my stride but soon after she left things deteriorated very quickly.

I think it is true that I had become dependent on my psychoanalytic therapist. Having someone to confide in on a weekly basis becomes like a crutch even if her treatment was actually pretty ineffective. I felt her departure keenly. This combined with my disappointment in my new job, my continued fixation on my ex, my hopeless approach to my medication and many other issues brought the pressure again to boiling point.

I think I had been at a wedding of a distant friend the weekend before, and I had drunk way too much and slept badly. My intrusive thoughts about paedophilia were particularly disturbing at this point as a close relation of mine had just had a baby who I saw frequently and who became a symbol in terms of this particular intrusive thought. On the Monday I took the day off work and spent it in bed. Late in the afternoon I got up, wrote a suicide note and took an overdose of my medication. As soon as I took those pills I knew that I had made a mistake. I called a relative who came and took me to A&E at the local hospital. I was out for twenty-four hours or so – I have no idea what happened between leaving my flat and waking up the next day.

I know it is a cliché but I truly think that it was a cry for help more than anything else. I was simply fed up with dealing with this stuff by myself and wanted somebody else to take over; I don't think I ever really meant to go through with it. I was later told by my OCD specialist that statistically OCD sufferers are not known to have high suicide rates. This makes sense to me. I was in a very bad way but there was a part of me that knew that my intrusive thoughts were just thoughts (however upsetting) and this same part still had hope that things would be different one day.

Recovery

When I came round to consciousness I met the duty psychiatrist in the hospital. She was very interested in my story so far and reassured me that I was not a failure but had actually done really well by coping so well up to this point. She also gave me hope that I had not come to the end of the line with my treatment, saying that I had tried only a handful of treatments in the armoury of modern science and that there were many more options that I could now consider in the treatment of my OCD. I also explained that I had found the side effects associated with the tricyclic antidepressant quite stressful, so she arranged a meeting with another psychiatrist who would assess whether there was a more suitable medication for me.

Shortly after this I was assessed by another NHS psychiatrist in a dilapidated mental health unit; she was young but was competent enough. She prescribed me another drug from the SSRI family. At last I had found my medication! It had no obvious side effects and it succeeded in maintaining my mood at a level that avoided me slipping back into depression and enabled me to better concentrate my treatment. Again I was not massively responsible when it came to taking the medication but it certainly worked. At the same time I was also given a course of CBT therapy on the NHS, but the psychologist was a generalist and was still undergoing training. It felt sometimes that I knew more about OCD than he did. However, he did help me in one way because I requested that he gave me some research papers of up-to-the-minute research into OCD. The research was amazing to read – these researchers were grappling with matters of direct relevance to my experiences. In the end I took the matter into my own hands and emailed one of the researchers directly. He responded and gave me a recommendation of a psychiatrist who specialized in the treatment of OCD and who practised not far from where I lived.

At last I had found a specialist in the treatment of my illness! It had taken four years and thousands of pounds wasted in paying people who simply were not qualified to treat OCD! Nevertheless, I got there eventually and it was inspirational to find somebody who had treated hundreds of patients with my illness. He had seen it all before, describing the subject matter of my intrusive thoughts as being run of the mill – I think he used the words 'as common as a cold'. I was truly elated. He was a no-nonsense kind of guy, not interested in pandering to me or talking about areas which he did not think were relevant to the task at hand. He had a number of fascinating insights into my form of OCD including the following:

1 Research has found that almost everybody has frequent, disturbing intrusive thoughts; the difference between those who are OCD sufferers and those who are not is that people with OCD attach responsibility

to their thoughts so that the moral nature of the thoughts is seen to be a personal reflection on them (a case of 'thought action fusion', as it is known). The OCD sufferer therefore attaches meaning to thoughts which a 'normal' person would treat as passing traffic. He gave a dramatic example of this when he said that at that precise moment he was thinking that he wished his children and his wife would die in a car crash on the way to the cinema tonight. I was amazed, he was completely relaxed, he had absolutely faith that a thought was really just that and that it had no relationship to reality. It resonated with me as I knew that I, of course, placed way too much importance on the content of my thoughts. By the way, as far as I know his kids are fine!

2 People who suffer from disturbing intrusive thoughts tend to have unrelenting moral standards (verging on intolerance) and the content of their thoughts tends to be the complete contradiction of these standards.

3 People with my form of OCD require certainty, i.e. they realize that thoughts don't necessarily cause actions but they want certainty that their intrusive thoughts would never play out to be correct. OCD sufferers lose a massive amount of energy in searching for this certainty, which simply cannot be found. It remains the case that to the best of his knowledge no convicted child abuser in UK prisons has ever been diagnosed with OCD. Does that mean it might never happen in the future? Of course it doesn't because the future is inherently uncertain.

4 People with OCD are often the safest people in the world. They are driven by a deep moral compass and

worry excessively about bad thoughts becoming a reality, but are overtly conscientious, sensitive and worried about harming anyone. He added that he would not think twice about asking me to babysit his kids and he was confident that I would look after them as well, if not better, than anyone else.

5 The physical effects which I experienced whilst having intrusive thoughts were not representative of sexual arousal but came about because of my association of the intrusive thoughts with danger, i.e. my body instinctively reacts as though I am exposed to danger, explaining the excess saliva, constricted throat and hairs standing on end.

6 He said that I needed to 'get a life', that I needed to spend less time concentrating on the 'irrational workings of the mind' and instead pay more attention to the outside world. I needed to refocus on tasks, hobbies or just the smell, touch and sights of the environment around me.

I was really excited each time I saw him as I felt that at last someone understood what was happening to me. Through him I also found an OCD support group that met near to my home (there are now well over thirty of such groups in the UK alone). He also suggested that I attend a conference dedicated to OCD and related anxiety disorders that was held once a year. It made such a difference to me to know that I was not alone.

The best thing about meeting this psychiatrist was that I now knew the type of treatment that suited me, which involved CBT specifically directed at OCD, including focusing on exposure to the content of my intrusive thoughts and 'getting out of my head' into the real world. I didn't need to go on searching anymore. At the same time it was tough going for, whilst I was particularly pumped up for the few days after seeing him, it was often difficult to maintain this level of enthusiasm as his words were difficult to hold on to. I also found myself sliding back to many of my old coping mechanisms – this was not surprising given how engrained they were after a lifetime of suffering from OCD.

In some respects you might say that a new battle begins once you have been diagnosed. My recovery definitely was not in a straight line and it felt sometimes like I was taking as many steps backward as I did forward. Also my ability to finance a renowned psychiatrist's fees was limited so my treatment probably lacked the coherence that it could have had. I was also still poorly disciplined when it came to taking my medication and I eventually came off it without any professional advice (not ideal!). It took a personal bereavement and a subsequent period of depression to get me focused again on really trying to address my OCD. I was also helped by the fact that I now had the strength that came from a loving and supportive relationship. She was the first person outside of my parents that I had really confided in. I told her everything. Despite my concerns to the contrary she was not shocked by any of my disclosures and said that she too had intrusive thoughts but just did not pay any attention to them. She did not judge me as I feared and her opinion of me did not change. In fact, I think that she was actually really impressed by how I had coped with my illness. Despite me fearing the worst, telling my girlfriend was actually one of the best things I could have done and her constant belief in me meant that I was able to again address my illness head on.

It was easier this time as I knew what I had to do. I went to see my doctor who put me back on the SSRI (I still take it to this day by the way); I also was recommended a new therapist by the psychiatrist who I had seen before (he no longer had time for new patients). We hit it off immediately, his style was very different to the psychiatrist but I found it no less inspirational. I have seen him every month or so ever since and I can honestly say that my ability to cope with my intrusive thoughts has improved massively. We have worked on a pretty structured programme including the following areas.

'Exposure' – this is a key area for treatment with people with intrusive thoughts. Just like people who have vertigo need exposure to heights to recover, people with intrusive thoughts need exposure to the content of their thoughts for them to become desensitized to them. So in my case the therapist and I put together an 'Anxiety Hierarchy' of different situations I would find increasingly uncomfortable. So for my intrusive thought about paedophilia, for example, the lowest level would be reading (rather than skipping) stories about paedophiles/paedophilia in the press and at the very top of the hierarchy was something like changing a baby's nappy. The idea is that you expose yourself to each situation and once you are comfortable with one you then rise further up the hierarchy. I found it to be very effective: I would certainly feel very anxious but after a while the anxiety would peak and then would start to decline. Sometimes I would resist a particular level and my internal dialogue would say, 'Be careful on this one, it could set you back'; it was, of course, the OCD speaking!

'De-ring-fencing' (my word not his!) – one of my problems is that I have always taken on board what the therapist says in general terms but when it comes to certain thoughts his words are met with my moral shutters crashing down. That is, I accept in general terms his logic about intrusive thoughts being the flotsam and jetsam of the mind which I can't control but when I come to a particularly upsetting intrusive thought I somehow exempt it from the rule as just being too morally reprehensible. The problem with this approach is that when you have ring-fenced a particular subject as being untouchable, you have given OCD an inch and it is clearly going to take a mile. As a result, the ring-fence can get bigger or another ring-fence can be set up around another thought in the future – it can quickly get out of hand for the simple reason that your brain, of course, does not understand what a ring-fence is. No thoughts should have a ring-fence around them because you can't control your thoughts, you can only control what you do.

My intrusive thoughts have not altogether gone and they can certainly come back, particularly if I am tired or run down. However, whereas I used to remonstrate with myself for hours or days after having a disturbing intrusive thought, I might now only do it for a few minutes. My treatment programme has enabled me to be much less controlled by my intrusive thoughts; my mind now finds it much harder to create lasting symbols around me to support or remind me of the subject of my intrusive thoughts; and I am less upset by the physical symptoms which are triggered by the intrusive thoughts. They still can happen, of course, but I now have a more plausible explanation for them. My therapist is very confident that I can be completely free of OCD. At the moment I have mostly good days and a few bad ones, but I think he might be right.

Postscript

As I wrote this piece I wrote down the advice that I would have liked to have received when I was grappling with my OCD. I hope that the following opinions are helpful to other sufferers and their families:

1 Question your treatment – in my experience if you have the right type of therapist for your OCD you will make rapid progress. If you are not making progress then you should not automatically blame yourself but question maybe whether you have been given poor advice. As my tortuous experience has proved many GPs and mental health practitioners unfortunately know very little about OCD. It remains the case that a very strong body of scientific research would indicate that a course of CBT with or without medication is the best way to treat OCD.

2 Private or NHS – I have always had the lucky position of being able to chose private treatment when the NHS did not work for me. Many people do not have this luxury. To these people I would say don't forget that you and your family are already paying for your healthcare through taxation. You have therefore already paid for your treatment; you have the right to be treated with respect, to receive

cutting-edge treatment and to be given choice if your current treatment is not working for you. Some NHS staff may forget it sometimes but they are ultimately there to deliver a service. I recognize that this confrontational stance can be difficult when your OCD is bad or you are feeling depressed, and I admit that in many areas of the country access to decent treatment is nothing less than scandalous, but I would urge you to at least keep this in mind –effective treatment should not be a luxury, it should be a right.

If you can afford private treatment then I would highly recommend it as it is easier to get hold of than treatment on the state, it takes away a lot of the stress associated with waiting lists and you are also often seen by more qualified people. At the start I found the fees really extortionate but with time I have started to view them as being more of an investment in me. A therapy session costs the same as a drunken night out. I know what I would rather have!

3 Take therapy seriously – you are either paying through the nose for it or you will have waited on a long waiting list to get it, so make the most of it. I sometimes found that I could not be bothered to do the homework and, like many people with mental health issues, I was often late for my sessions. Why? I have no idea! The only person who lost out in these scenarios was me. Prepare for your sessions beforehand, think of issues that you want to discuss, take notes of key points which are discussed and, better still, record the session so that you can listen to it

again. It is difficult to take away a great deal of what you will discuss in your fifty minutes, so at least give yourself a fighting chance.

4 Medication is not a bad thing – taking antidepressants still has a stigma associated with it. Many people, including doctors, will tell you that the ultimate goal is always to come off them. This is fine if they just don't work for you or if you have come off them with no adverse effects and managed to successfully maintain any improvement you made while on them, but if taking medication enables you to maintain an even keel and get on with your life then so what? I for one have often sought the goal of being off medication and have always found it to be a pyrrhic victory. I am now very happy to be on medication for the rest of my life.

5 There is a suitable medication out there for you – it took three attempts before I found the one most suitable to me. If you try a medication and it does not work as promised or has nasty side effects then you don't need to stay on it just because someone prescribed it to you. Go back to them and explain what is happening and ask them to look at other options of which there are bound to be plenty. Bear in mind also that developments are happening in this area all the time and recommendations may change over time. It is, of course, important to only move on to a new medication on the advice of a health professional – this transition needs to be managed carefully as one drug leaves your system and another one enters it.

6 Take your medication properly – as is painfully clear from my story I have always had a problem taking

my medication as I should. I think it is only since I have been with my wife that she has instilled in me the discipline to look after myself, including taking my medication as prescribed and always ensuring that I have a repeat prescription before I run out. Even a few days of not taking your medication can mean that physiologically you need to go back to scratch again. Don't forget that it is also extremely important that when you choose to come off medication that you do so slowly and with the help of a GP or other medical professional. Coming off quickly and without proper support can have catastrophic results.

7 Give some thought to who you tell about your intrusive thoughts – this is really down to personal preference and there is no right answer. On the one hand once you have been diagnosed it might feel liberating to tell the world about your intrusive thoughts. On the other, as was the case with me, you might feel that you would prefer to keep it relatively close. This is not because I was ashamed, but it is more the fact that I simply did not see the value that anyone else apart from the closest people to me (my parents, my wife and a few others) could really bring to my recovery from OCD. There may be no need to tell work colleagues or friends anything about it if you choose not to. I would try to find at least one person to confide in, though.

If you work and you need to go to frequent outpatient treatment appointments during office hours you might find it easier to confide in somebody in management or human resources to take the stress away. You probably won't actually need to go into much detail and they will be obliged to be reasonable. In my case, I have never felt the need to do this as my appointments have always been approximately one month apart, which is no more than most people take when they have routine doctor's, dentist's or hospital appointments. I have never had any issues with taking the time off to go to the 'doctors' so long as I have given the relevant people notice.

8 Consume alcohol in moderation – pharmaceutical companies will normally advise in the small print that alcohol should not be consumed whilst taking medication. Speak to your doctor but in my experience most doctors say that moderation is the key, not total abstinence. Don't forget also that alcohol is a depressant and has a whole host of other side effects. If you are fighting a war against disturbing intrusive thoughts the last thing you want to do is to deliberately handicap yourself.

9 Exercise – one of my therapists once said to me that exercise is the 'unsung hero of mental health treatment'. I certainly have always found it so and throughout my recovery I have exercised regularly. Cardiovascular exercise is the best in my opinion and there is certainly quite a bit of research to suggest that it naturally increases the serotonin levels in the brain, which are associated with greater happiness. I always go for a swim or a run as a general pick-me-up if I am feeling a bit down: it never fails to make me feel better. Team sports are particularly good, of course, because they involve

exercise and social interaction but they are not always practical.

10 Keep busy – if you can, try to work. In my case the discipline of work, the social interaction and the opportunities to become engrossed in something that is not my OCD have been instrumental in my recovery. People with OCD often feel that they need to spend time by themselves working through their thoughts and that is why they can't work. Nothing, in my opinion, could be further from the truth.

If your mental health problems are so severe that full-time work is just impossible then perhaps try part-time charity work or take up some hobbies. I am sure you will not regret it.

Post Postscript

I would like to dedicate this piece to my parents and my wife who have been such pillars of support during my illness. My parents' determination to find appropriate treatment was resolute even when my hope was fading. They have also never made me doubt their love and their patience, and their wise counsel has helped me through the most difficult times. My wife has always made it easy for me to talk to about my intrusive thoughts even if I sometimes find the subject matter uncomfortable. Her deep understanding of how I work has made our relationship even stronger. You will no doubt have read or will read in OCD literature that many psychologists (not very helpfully!) state that sufferers can find it hard to maintain relationships; it is probably the case that living with OCD makes lasting relationships more difficult, but

I would like to reassure the reader that it is certainly possible to enjoy serious and lasting relationships with the condition and that these can be a very positive influence on your recovery.

7

69 ways to cope with OCD

As I'm still dealing with OCD on a daily basis – and refusing to feel a failure for not having vanquished it – I have devoted this story to my 69 idiosyncratic coping strategies.

So, here are some of the ways in which I've attempted to escape the OCD cerebral straitjacket, in case they are useful:

1 As soon as you awake each morning, state loudly: 'I am not only marvellous, but sane!' If you're an insomniac say it once an hour, but don't wake other people as they might disagree with you.
2 A mordant sense of humour is invaluable, but be circumspect. My husband is a literal-minded scientist and now pours himself a stiff drink before enquiring about my day.
3 If you think that your therapist is rubbish, chances are they are. Save money and ditch them; don't forget to cut them out of your Will. If you're a man in love with your female therapist, turn up to your next session in a Mankini (*Borat*) and she will terminate the relationship for you.

4 Did Ms Jeffers – she who rashly wrote *Feel the Fear and Do It Anyway* – have OCD? Discuss (*10 marks*).

Avoid over-compensating for your normal fearfulness by feeling obliged to do everything you're scared of. OCD-sufferers already slay dragons on a daily basis, even if just making Toad in the Hole. So, absolutely no need to wander around Peckham council estates at 2 a.m. to prove how brave* you are. Anyway, you'll frighten the residents.

5 You've merely got OCD, you are not insane: this is both disappointing and reassuring. Now you can choose whether to:

- wax evangelical about enlightening the masses and wave a megaphone around outside the Halifax; or
- lie on the sofa cuddling a sack of Maltesers, smugly watching *House* and knowing Dr Greg House *is* nuts.

6 Categorize, alliteratively, a couch-full of psychiatrists (*10 marks*).

I haven't experienced psychiatry, but found psychotherapy useful for helping me to gain a real, if precarious, sense of self. Find someone professionally qualified (of course) and who also isn't a charlatan on other levels. Otherwise, it's akin to ushering a stranger into your home whilst you are *déshabillé*. Your head space contains valuable and fragile artefacts, even if it does currently feel like a skip.

---

* For 'brave' read reckless.

7 Endeavour not to be superstitious about religion, i.e. don't flinch and glance upwards when you blaspheme. Conversely, it could be a good move to give up irritating God for Lent.

8 Don't take on everybody else. If the truck driver is also having a bad hair day he *will* run over your bicycle, probably with you still on it. You are then entitled to wish OCD on him.

9 Don't punish yourself and, yes, tattoos do come under 'self-harm'. Particularly when you have the wretched things lasered off, because you're fed up with:

- your GP snorting with laughter;
- the cartoon turtle genuinely having a wrinkled neck;
- being reminded of Damian every time you have a shower;
- Celtic symbols (so passé);
- agog Japanese tourists perusing the Kanji symbols on your arm.

10 What's the point of worrying? Discuss (*10 marks*).
   If it's about someone else, what is the point of two people being unhappy instead of only one? It's positively selfish to wallow, when misery ripples outwards and affects others, too. Don't worry – be happy!

11 Lie on the therapist's couch – as opposed to underneath it. Try not to sit bolt upright on the edge for fifty minutes, still wearing your duffle-coat – it makes the therapist want to take up smoking.

12 If you're scared of shutting the cat in the fridge, take it to an auction. People quite often buy white goods.

13 Weeping can act as an invaluable safety valve. Try and avoid a public session though when you don't have the following to bawl into:

- loo paper;
- tissues;
- an attractive stranger's handkerchief;
- a pre-shrunk shoulder.

Also avoid sobbing:

- when you have a cold;
- while wearing contact lenses;
- if there isn't an appreciative audience;
- prior to a social function. Otherwise the hosts will assume you come from a broken home/marriage or are allergic to their children.

14 If cleaning is your vocation and you can be found at 8 a.m. on a Sunday morning vacuuming out the bread-bin, don't let your flatmates take advantage.

15 Best not to talk about a particular anxiety to someone while you're panicking about it – unless they're a paid professional, in which case that's what they're there for. Wait for remission – 24 hours perhaps: we're not talking *Waiting for Godot* here, although it might feel like it. You could then find yourself broaching the issue in a calmer way, if at all.

16 Conversely, don't allow anxiety to build up; let it out in bite-sized chunks – otherwise the stress can make

exam nerves pale into insignificance. It's not a good look – exploding (see Mr Creosote in *The Meaning of Life*.)

17 Be realistic. You might be nervously convinced that you're powerful enough to destroy Oxford Street crowds with a sigh – chance would be a fine thing. Look in a mirror: you're 5ft 1in. with a bad back.

18 Don't avoid people if you suddenly visualize yourself stabbing them without good reason, or your friends will think it's something *they've* done. If you are convinced you'll pinion Archibald to the work-surface, stop sharpening the bread-knife and hire a hitman. This prevents all sorts of legal problems, such as getting caught.

19 Remember: it's comfortingly rare for people with OCD to perform the violent acts which cerebrally torment us so. Ergo, we are often lovely, caring individuals –particularly in light of all that temptation. Unlike Pinochet. Time to give yourself an Oprah Hug.

20 Coming out: I would recommend confiding the fact that you have OCD to people you trust and feel close to. Be prepared (I was a Girl Guide for three weeks, it shows) and have handy:

- hip flask;
- tissues;
- flak jacket;
- medical dictionary;
- one of those ceramic phrenological heads so beloved by the Victorians and pretentious antique shops;

- Magic Markers, if you believe a phrenological head is relevant, or you are Artistic.

Explain *briefly* how OCD affects you, or your confidante will wonder if they have spinach in their teeth as you stare fixedly at them. It also helps to point out that you're not mad, as you tap the chair/the budgerigar/their nose seven times.

21 Remember: other people have problems, too. If they're concealing them, they're just not as brave as you are.

22 These same people might be silently sympathetic when they see you muttering in Morrisons, working up the courage to pick up a newspaper. Don't assume that onlookers are necessarily hostile, just because you are revisiting the hideous self-consciousness of adolescence. They're probably brooding about the lack of Quorn-flavoured crisps and haven't even noticed you twitching by the magazine rack.

22 It is incredibly altruistic of you to suffer so as to provide a career for therapists and medical staff. Remind them at your next appointment that they'd be sleeping in a doorway if it wasn't for you.

22 Write down brief details of the worry of the moment, then put the note somewhere safe and try to forget it for a while. This gives you a modicum of control. If you don't want to think about it again, wear earplugs* and set fire to the piece of paper.

23 Utilize bloody-minded determination – 'I'm British for God's sake!' At least a stiff upper lip means you

---

* Because of the smoke alarm.

won't need anti-wrinkle cream. If you resemble Mick Jagger, starch your moustache.

24 Give self pep-talks, in the manner of a bossy head-mistress. These are incredibly effective in the rush-hour: you can sometimes get a whole carriage, never mind a seat.

25 Go for long walks. Don't forget hymn-sheet, vest, map and reluctant dog. Avoid mountains – you're not Julie Andrews.

26 Play Chess, it's great for tidying up loose ends of anxiety. Perhaps not *so* beneficial for those of us who are competitive, but also bad losers. After crossly losing a game of Chess to a very desirable man, I couldn't lure him to the Centrepoint restaurant as planned. He wouldn't get in the lift; he said he wasn't being trapped on the twenty-third floor near me, windows and sharp cutlery. To make matters worse, as Achilles turned on his heel, he skidded on a bishop and we ended up at A&E instead. The relationship never recovered: he married the male nurse.

27 Exercise your atrophied *Senseofself* muscle. You are courageous and resourceful – be selfish, take risks. Don't check anything for 24 hours.

Following day: Am I right, or am I right? You're still alive and so are most of the people you've met.

28 Give your OCD a name – unfortunately mine's called Ormerod. (Don't get me wrong: I wanted David Beckham, but he was rearranging his sock-drawer.) Ormerod is a nagging, fearful and occa-sionally embarrassing companion with a comb-over. Tastefully attired in a 1970s woollen tank top,

Crimplene slacks and polished shoes, he lived with his mother until she died in suspicious circumstances. To keep Ormerod quiet, I should maintain a personal space of 100 yards. He would like me to wear a hooded Babygro with mittens, so as not to absent-mindedly pick at my skin or pinch the postman. If I upset Ormerod, he rummages in his ears with a biro and turns nasty. Suffice to say that his philosophy sucks.

29 Breathe deeply. Don't get me started, I can't do this – when I try I resemble a Guppy on hot sand.

30 Don't let other people tell you how you feel – you're the one living it.

31 Look up at the sky to clear your mind, but not when stepping off the kerb. I also find visualizing an empty cardboard box works wonders, but it may just be that I'm coming to terms with future accommodation.

32 Imagine you are reassuring someone else, for example a child, when you're having a difficult time.

33 Read fiction, but not Jeffrey Archer. Better still, write a bestselling gory thriller.

34 At the risk of being labelled a kill-joy ... avoid fleeing unwelcome thoughts via promiscuity or drugs, including alcohol. It's awfully tiring and even Usain Bolt couldn't run that fast for that long. You'll also jump awake at 4 a.m. in agonies of embarrassment if you make it to adulthood.

35 Be pragmatic: if it's going to take fifteen minutes to leave the house, give yourself a break occasionally and allow for it. Personally I need to check: the cats' welfare, iron, taps, plugs, lights, cooker and whether

the kitchen tap has come unscrewed at the base. One therapist got quite snappy when I revealed that due to my husband's Zen-like approach to DIY it *is* possible in my house for the wash-basin to drop off the wall and for loops of electric cable to be crocheted together with domino connectors, forming a noose perilously close to the top of our rickety staircase with a couple of steps missing . . .

36 No one died utilizing a public lavatory – but I'll bet someone did because they didn't (see Mr Creosote, again).

37 Congratulate yourself on being so concerned for other people's safety: you are an old-fashioned, empathic and civilized individual.

38 Stare up at the stars, admire the lugubrious moon and meditate on how insignificant your problems are. If living in Hounslow go somewhere *sans* light pollution, like Northumberland.

39 Dinosaurs were probably equally anguished: at least you have an opposable thumb and can write poetry. Avoid doggerel like this though:

OCD & I

I've got OCD;
Doesn't mean
I'm out of my tree.
But
Damocles' sword
Hangs over me.

I'm just obsessive
And depressive
Deeeeply
Caring and compulsive
A fully-rounded
Person.
Me!

40 In polite society, only one's doctor uses the word 'anal'.

41 Keep a mole-wrench in the bathroom so that guests can turn on the taps.

42 Turn your ability to foresee disaster to your advantage, in a lucrative career! Consider applying to be Health and Safety Consultant for Tower Hamlets, or a barrister specializing in causality. Alternatively pen *Old Moore's Almanac for the New Millennium* and make a fortune appearing on breakfast TV.

43 If you must kill people, join the armed forces.

44 Insist your fiancé/e signs a prenuptial agreement. This states that they love you and 'Ormerod' and will hand over two-thirds of their estate to you both, in the event of divorce. (Why do *you* think people with OCD are statistically more likely to celebrate their Platinum Anniversary than their brethren?)

45 My school maths teacher would have been astonished by my current proficiency at mental arithmetic. If, like me, you count things in groups, pat yourself on the back + back + back and add numerical skill to your CV. As you are a multitasking phenomenon, you might also wish to include your

expertise in the following areas* but be cognisant that colleagues may feel inadequate:

- Hygiene
- Eating disorders
- Tourette's syndrome
- Arson
- Fascinating phobias
- Flash-flooding
- Hoarding.

Perhaps it's best to just type 'versatile'.

46 When checking things as I leave home, I find it currently helps if I give each item a number and say it aloud as I mentally tick it off, as in: washing-machine turned off, '1'; taps off, '2', and so on . . . If you reach '50', if you're not in insurance risk-assessment, you should be. If my litany reaches a higher number than planned, it's because I'm re-checking. I then valiantly *just go out*. And I try not to creep back home from the bus-stop ten minutes later to check I haven't left the oven on.

47 Rather than repeatedly testing the lock by endeavouring to wrench your front door off the hinges each time you leave home – then hovering anxiously in the porch for twenty minutes waiting for the door to fall off – employ a notebook and tick things off. The pen is mightier than panic, unless . . .

48 . . . like me, you're a writer who is phobic about pens. In which case, ask a friend un-phased by a

---

*Delete as appropriate.

sterile environment to go round after you've left for work and photograph locks and sockets, and then email you the pictures.

49 Don't get sacked for staring at close-ups of electric sockets on your screen.

50 Be bendy, not brittle – think wrought as opposed to cast iron. Remember the Tay Bridge Disaster? Neither do I. This analogy isn't about emulating Old Iron Lady Thatcher, but recognizing when you're tense and devising strategies to relax your body and thoughts. A friend found Yoga very helpful so I tried it, but my muscles locked in an embarrassing position and the instructor had to call a cab. I'm still wearing the leotard.

51 Think positive; ubiquitous CCTV camera coverage means you don't need to keep looking behind you in the street. Chances are that if you *have* poked that businessman's eye out with your umbrella, someone will have seen you. (Obviously not him, whose eye you have just removed . . .) This is the only positive thing I shall say about CCTV, as it's bad enough neurotically performing some daft ritual without suspecting there's also a camera recording your actions. Infringement of fidgeting liberties, I call it.

52 Are you still prone to looking behind you to check whether you kicked away someone's white stick, or stuffed a baby in a litter bin? Avoid whiplash by installing a small mirror above the right eye – perhaps hanging rakishly from your cycling helmet or a hair grip. Flaunted with enough *savoir faire*, people will enviously assume it's a fashion accessory or an anti-mugging device.

53 Blame your parents (Philip Larkin based a career on it):

- The sound-track to my 1960s childhood was not: 'She loves you, yeah yeah yeah', but my mother shouting, 'You'll have someone's eye out!' as I obediently endeavoured to balance peas on a fork. That woman has a lot to answer for.
- Censure your parents if they are prone to OCD – they *chose* to be role models.

Helpful Tip for Adolescents: suggest at family gatherings that authoritarian parenting instigates OCD. You'll be allowed to do things your mates can only dream of: Wrinklies will ignore a lot to avoid forking out for therapy.

54 Punch pillows: it's an effective way of releasing pent-up anger and also unhooks tense shoulders from earlobes. Recommended for parents with truculent teenagers. Wear a mask if you're allergic to feathers or are feeling frisky.

55 If the thought makes you yawn, go to sleep – but not face-down on your computer keyboard after lunch.

56 The world doesn't revolve around you.

57 Don't aspire to sainthood – you're only a normal, sinning human.

58 Set a legal precedent. I don't think anyone has been divorced yet for clandestinely turning off their wife's radio alarm so that she's late for work for a month, on the grounds that it'll set fire to the bedroom. Then again, perhaps the Old Testament prophets had OCD. Fear of floods, plague, authority, fire . . . ? It all sounds reassuringly familiar and might help your divorce case.

59 Go for a run, but not near me. I can walk faster in kitten heels than most of the sweaty joggers who lumber helplessly behind me all the way to Victoria, panting on my neck. In fact I shall garrotte the next one with my Prada handbag.

60 Capitalize on being a Control Freak:

(a) Manage your family with an iron rod. The benefits are that this:

- stops costly teenagers overstaying their welcome;
- enables you to make a profit renting out their room;
- allows you to throw exhilarating parties, instead of tip-toeing around in revision silence;
- means your husband will leave you, *at last*, for a younger woman;
- enables you to do exactly as you like ... (Cue Christopher Lee evil laugh.)

(b) Micro-manage work colleagues – everything from their dress-code, to the correct way in which to order new photocopier paper. The latter particularly infuriates administrators, but popularity is overrated. The benefits:

- if it doesn't get you sacked, you'll be promoted;
- either way, you'll have an enjoyable and fulfilling time.

61 Market yourself properly: you don't have OCD, you're a Perfectionist.

62 Treat your body as a million-pound Belgravia property, not a defunct village bus-shelter. It's easier to cope with OCD if you're healthy.

63 Join a gym (see No. 62) with a punchbag and BHIs (Buffed and Hot Instructors). This promotes healthy hormonal activity and joyous endorphin overload as you lift weights. You already run for the bus, so by-pass the running machine and head for the sauna. This regime produces smugness and a beautiful body, leading to envy and dislike being manifested by friends. Hence the need for endorphins. On second thoughts, selflessly stay at home consuming cake on the sofa and watching old episodes of *Ugly Betty*, in order that friends aren't unnecessarily upset. They will thank you.

64 Murderous fantasies are a *sane* response to your nose becoming jammed in someone's armpit or the train doors in the rush-hour. Nevertheless it's a good idea to remind yourself, when experiencing an OCD Hammer Horror movie, that it's only Ormerod having a bit of fun (or Barbarella or Gawain or Sigourney Weaver – whatever rocks your carriage). You know the fantasy where you're Ms Weaver and ripping that man's head off, because his elbow is hogging your arm-rest at 35,000 feet? Emerge *quickly*, or you'll spend the rest of the flight to New York squinting at your plump neighbour out of the corner of your eye and checking your sleeve for bloodstains, while he wonders with increasing excitement whether you're about to proposition him. This can lead to a diplomatic incident.

65 If you're concerned about the environment, practice

anger-management on a rowing machine connected to the National Grid – or row somewhere.

66 Avoid academic work. When my brain is honed, I could gain a PhD in Worry inside a month. (Best not to let your teenage offspring read this: any excuse not to swot for GCSEs.)

67 It's healthy, not unfaithful, to express admiration for attractive people. I recommend doing this on a first date to see what happens.

68 Study for qualifications in Psychotherapy or Psychiatry. Let's face it, most practitioners are barking, so you'll have a head start – *not* being mad.

Finally:

69 Don't rely on others for reassurance: be independent and sign up for a course of CBT (Costly Beautiful Treats). In the immortal words of L'Oreal: 'You're worth it!'

69 (a) Now cut up your credit cards.

8

Against the odds: from OCD bondage to freedom

Thwack! Thwack! Thwack! The pain surged through my bum in waves as my public school housemaster smugly sheathed his birch. He probably thought he'd taught me a lesson, but I wasn't so sure. If that's how he thought to teach me discipline, or respect for my elders or team spirit, I'd prove him wrong for I was a stubborn lad and, in getting back at the school, I would really be getting back at my father . . .

Fitting in with the school's ethos was the last thing on my mind. Concealing my (then undiagnosed) illness from the other boys and masters was a full-time job which meant that my studies also had to take a back seat. Everything and everybody came second to my all-consuming obsessions and compulsions. Why couldn't they understand that? No doubt because I hadn't told them. I didn't *dare* tell them; I felt far too guilty and ashamed to do that.

'It seems to me,' wrote my father to an eminent specialist in the summer of 1948, 'that the boy has been browbeaten at both his schools. He has a highly developed sense of guilt, fear and self-doubt and my wife sums up his tension as due to a fear of failure.'

But even if I had blown my cover, the boys in my school house wouldn't have understood. I didn't understand it myself and felt the stupidest person on the planet. I could only sit back and wonder how it was that life came so easily to the other boys; they seemed instinctively to know how to function and even be happy, without rubbing authority – or their peers – up the wrong way.

Fighting for praise

What was their secret? What was that mysterious gravitational pull that the popular boys so effortlessly exercised over the others? Being so needy and hungry for peer approval, I desperately needed to know the answer. Why did I have to fight so hard for every scrap of praise and approval? I tried flattery, but that didn't work. I tried jokes, but the laughter quickly turned to sniggers. Yet, if it worked for the popular boys; why not for me? Obviously, because I was stupid. Even the Master himself appeared to agree.

Survival was the name of the game – but on my terms, not theirs. I felt like an oil tanker that wasn't for turning; I couldn't change course just to fit in with some abstract school ethos. Trying to conform was more painful than the punishments I incurred by not conforming. I realized, of course, that to conform was the fast track to acceptance, and acceptance was what I desperately sought and needed. I was ruinously conflicted since the price of conforming was to drive a coach-and-horses through my even stronger compulsive need to obsess. I had a relentless need to organise and control my possessions. My OCD, in other words, was stronger even than my yearning for peer acceptance. I found this interior battle physically exhausting. Something had to give – and it did.

At war with myself

With the Second World War just ended, the pressure to conform was intense. Had not discipline won us the war? Wasn't that, therefore, the all-purpose remedy for insubordination? The sight of my birch-striped bum doubtless discouraged my roommates from any thought of rebellion. For them at least, it was too high a price to pay for non-conformity . . .

My appalling end-of-term reports were used as a stick to beat me with – as much to justify the school's hardline approach as to keep my unwitting parents onside. Ill? How could I be? Did I not look the picture of health and had I not sailed through my Common Entrance exam and did I not have the makings of a demon bowler on the cricket field?

Knocked into shape

In that martial post-war culture, mental illness was too often seen as a cop-out, the coward's escape route. Hadn't they already seen enough of that, with young men trying to avoid enlistment in the war? No, no, I was not ill, merely dreamy, introverted and unpardonably stubborn. They'd make a man of me yet. My parents were not to worry; were they not paying good money to have me knocked into shape? All I had to do was pull my socks up – or have them pulled up for me . . . So no psychiatrist was wheeled in; indeed, I'm not even sure the school had one.

Instead, those disapproving termly reports continued to land on my worried parents' laps.

Remarrying in his early fifties, my father wanted a quiet life and no children. My mother, an American twenty years his junior, did very much want children. As it was a love-match, my father, ever the Yorkshire gentleman, gave way and had me and, two years later, my sister.

The quiet life was to prove elusive as my father had inadvertently built a house directly under the flight path of Germany's warplanes. Although not an OCD sufferer himself, he did have an obsessive personality and his idea of a nightmare was to have a noisy tearaway toddler smearing sticky fingers over his prized antiques.

An English country gentleman, my father was gentleness, integrity and loyalty personified. He had, however, been damaged in his turn by an authoritarian father and his life was disciplined and routine-led – hardly the ideal soulmate for a lively and inquisitive son.

Having lived through two world wars, my father was almost as much a disciplinarian as my school housemaster. Being so much younger and on alien soil, my mother deferred to my father's somewhat idiosyncratic take on child-rearing. Children were, on the whole, to be seen and not heard, and shown off to the neighbours at teatime.

Bubble-wrapped

More plaintive than angry, my father's constant refrain was: 'Don't touch that!' It was as if my father treated me like an untamed dog, safe only when on a leash, and so I was ludicrously ill-prepared for life in the outside world.

Even riding a bike on the (then almost empty) roads was considered dangerous and I only got pedalling after many a tearful pleading with my parents. There were few local children to play with as most were considered 'too rough'. Yes, there was a garden to play in, but there was little point kicking a ball if there were no one of your own age to kick it back.

The nearby farm also beckoned, but our parents considered that the cowpats in the field would mean more hand-washing and that the quagmire by the end gate spelt 'Danger'. Life, in short, had become crucifyingly frustrating and I lived in a constant state of ill-suppressed anger. I felt as if life itself had become a no-go area.

Suffocated by this no-win battery-hen existence, my sister and I rebelled. I enjoyed stealing half-crowns from my father's dressing table as he snored his way through the night. I also enjoyed smoking Craven A and Players cigarettes in bed but, annoyingly, this did not bother my father – so I promptly stopped.

Freedom at last!

The more our parents disapproved of our childhood pranks, the more we enjoyed them. Rebellion, we found, was fun and a bit of an adventure. Indeed, it was that early taste of freedom that later enabled me to survive prep school more or less intact.

But public school was a different matter. By the age of fourteen, I'd become a secretive and all but unmanageable school outcast, given to sudden uncontrollable fits of rage. My belligerence was further fuelled by having to try to deal with my OCD. Criticism of my 'anti-social' behaviour by grown-ups seemed to me to be plain stupid since it showed how incapable they were of understanding me. Survival was key and anyone crossing my path got short shrift.

And, if my behaviour was termed 'anti-social' then so much the better. That was a bonus and one of my few remaining sources of pleasure; getting back at authority gave me a real buzz and it felt good to give those grown-ups a taste of the hurt that they had landed on me. There was no point trying to explain all this to my father as he'd never have understood.

Broken toys

By the age of fourteen I no longer needed my father to mend my toys – as a child, I had thought this ability was the only good thing about him. But now that I felt I had nothing to lose and no reason to be polite to him anymore, I was free at last to be as anti-social as I wanted.

After yet another row with him, I reinforced the message by hurling downstairs two of his treasured antique dining chairs. The sound of them breaking up on the wooden floor below was music to my ears. My – still undiagnosed – illness was fuelled by my hatred of my father and by the constraints he unwittingly placed on my mother's freedom to express her love for me.

Posting a letter

Having just come through the 1939–45 war, my poor father now faced the prospect of a different type of battle – on the *domestic* front. I found posting a letter a nightmare as it triggered my gut-wrenching fear of losing things. It wasn't enough just to post a letter as others did. Before releasing the letter, I had to wait for the traffic noise to still so that I could hear it fall to the bottom of the box.

Even if I'd heard my letter land, I'd still have to feel inside the box with my hand to ensure that it hadn't got stuck at the top. And, as if that weren't enough, I'd have to scrutinize every paving stone around the box to convince myself that it hadn't, despite all my checks, accidentally fallen on to the street. Imagine the embarrassment of my uncomprehending father as he stood helplessly by, watching his fourteen-year-old son's bizarre behaviour being acted out in public.

He reckoned that my pathological fear of losing possessions stemmed from my first year in prep school, when a boy stole some trinket from my locker to which, for some reason, I attached great importance. And imagine, too, my sixty-seven-year-old father's feelings as he bore silent witness to his son's more protracted rituals inside the house. Eventually, the whole family became complicit in 'freeing' me – albeit temporarily – from the iron grip of my obsessive thinking, which had suddenly hit them out of the blue. I demanded that my family repeat certain ritual phrases in a way that could 'release' me from the barbed hooks of my obsessive thoughts.

OCD's inner logic

I found relative peace among the private possessions in my former nursery toy cupboard. But even these held me in thrall as I could only enjoy them if they were placed exactly so on the shelves. My aim in doing this was to avoid the discomfort or, at worst, mental anguish that would result from my not doing so. Within the OCD bubble it is that logic which prevails. Not to have gone along with it would have struck me as crazy since the lack of order on those shelves would have caused me so much pain. OCD has its own logic. That is why, for those outside the bubble, like my father, it was as pointless to discuss my problems logically as it had been pointless for the school to throw its ethos at me. Neither made the slightest impact. OCD, like heroin or alcohol, overrides all reason.

I was ruled, among other things, by my possessions. Sharing them – or, indeed, anything else – with someone was anathema to me as it represented loss; I needed them to be mine and mine alone. Possessing the key to my toy cupboard therefore had huge symbolic value for me.

Whether locked away or not, all of my other possessions had to be arranged in a certain way. I couldn't get to bed, never mind to sleep, unless, for instance, my clothes and slippers were ordered just so – which could have taken half an hour to get right. The counterpane, too, had to fit squarely over the bed before I could allow myself even to think of sleep.

Types of 'loss'

Obsessive thoughts had to be 'cleared' before I could allow myself to fully relax. I might, for instance, find myself stuck – like the proverbial stuck record – over something I'd regretted doing, or not doing, during the day. Such mistakes had to be rationalized out of existence with some verbal formula, which, by dint of endless repetition, had to be got exactly right.

If, for instance, I'd messed up a job interview, I'd try to exorcise the pain of guilt and regret by magically 'making it right' by reasoning that I might still land the job despite my poor showing; that, if I didn't get it, it wouldn't really matter; that, if I *had* landed the job, I might live to regret it; that I must work out how better to present myself at any subsequent interview; that maybe I should contact the successful candidate and ask him or her to give me their formula for success; that failing the interview could prove to be a blessing in disguise as, come to think of it, my prospective boss looked a bit judgmental and not very creative . . .

It was only when I could drum up enough good reasons for seeing my messed-up interview in a positive, rather than in a negative, light that I could free myself from the hook of tortured self-blame. The more obvious my mistake or failure, the denser had to be the coat of rationalization needed to transform it, as if by magic, into a cause for celebration. With all guilt and regret finally banished, I was free once again to move on and live like everyone else – until, that is, the next obsession loomed.

And then there was the forgotten or misremembered item from my mental 'to do' list – another potent form of 'loss'. For example, I may have forgotten that putting out a pair of socks for the morning was on my 'to do' list – I would know that something was missing from the list but I wouldn't know exactly what it was. The aim here was not to 'make the loss right', but simply to recall to memory the mislaid thought or item. I could sometimes spend hours 'getting it back'. Failure, with its concomitant admission of defeat, would bring acute and continuing discomfort since there could be no closure and no hiding place from reality.

Success, on the other hand, would bring the usual wave of release, which curiously bore no resemblance to the importance of the 'lost' item. Its importance, however, lay not so much in itself as in the discovery that a really important item had *not* been lost. Failure to retrieve, say, a particular thought breeds the nagging uncertainty that something important – a diary item, an appointment time – *had* been forgotten.

The search for respite

While in that state of near-mental paralysis, I couldn't focus on my own healthier concerns, never mind on those of others. The search for some respite in this double-bind world I inhabited took precedence over everything and everybody else. To assume otherwise would be to expect a drowning man to worry about his neighbour's migraine.

If that was hell, then heaven for me had always been my bed, my ultimate refuge. Seventh heaven was consuming my pitifully small ration of sweets and gobbling up stacks of musty adventure books, bought, when I was still able to go out, from second-hand booksellers. Give me a stirring book and I would be off to the South Seas on the wings of my latest adventure.

Little Hitler

As my OCD worsened around my fifteenth birthday, I didn't dare leave the house for fear of losing something outside. Then it was my bedroom I couldn't leave for fear of losing something in the house. So it was my *bed* that beckoned so seductively when I could no longer eat with my parents and sister in the downstairs dining room. After bringing up my meals to me on a tray, I would need them to wring their hands to prove to me that they were taking nothing from the room when they left. Before giving the tray back, I had to put myself through a far more rigorous ritual that involved my shaking each dirty plate and piece of cutlery several times as proof that none of my possessions remained stuck to them.

My bewildered father didn't know whether he was coming or going. The war he could cope with, but this . . . I had become a little Hitler and my father warned my mother against over-indulging me and in this, at least, he was probably right.

There is a delicate balance to be struck here between constructive and counter-productive help and I will return to this grey area later. My parents had finally come to realize that the problem was bigger than they, or the school, could manage and that I was, after all, in urgent need of psychiatric help.

Smoke-filled silence

It was shortly after my fifteenth birthday that a top Wimpole Street paediatrician finally diagnosed my illness as something called obsessive compulsive disorder (OCD). We were none the wiser, of course, but it was comforting to have a label attached to my condition and to know that I wasn't the only one in the world with it.

My doctor was a pipe-smoking OCD specialist paediatrician and was thought to know all there was to know about the disorder. However, instead of describing the symptoms and treatment that I would finally stumble across at a later age, he drew a link between my OCD and masturbation! I didn't have a clue what he was talking about but decided that silence was the best policy and continued to see him for a period of six months. However, far from improving, my illness had worsened. Unable to tolerate losing thoughts or possessions, I now found myself unable to tolerate losing *myself*.

The minute I began losing myself in a film or adventure book, I had to pull back into the 'reality' of my obsessional comfort zone. In the end, the fear of losing myself got so bad that I made it an iron rule to ration my daily book-reading to a single page. After being mercifully withdrawn from my baffled paediatrician, I was promptly despatched to another one, who also got short shrift after failing to make any headway with me. And so to a third, and then to a fourth. It should be said in all fairness that they gave up on me as much as my family and I gave up on them.

Besides, all those weekly medical trips were starting to prove expensive. Being by this stage too ill to travel by train or bus, a taxi had to be hired to drive me the forty miles to and from London. It was, alas, the only option as petrol rationing prevented my father from driving me there himself.

Nightmare diagnosis

A tremendous shock was about to hit us. My doctors, so powerless to help me, came to the collective view that only surgical intervention could 'save' me. They recommended the treatment of last resort, normally only recommended for would-be suicides – a pre-frontal leucotomy on my brain. In the 1940s, that still experimental procedure was crude and risky. If it went wrong – or even only half-right –

it could leave me festering for the rest of my life in a mental institution.

My mother – who, up to that point had loyally deferred to my father's management of my case – blew her top. No way would she allow her son's brain to be invaded with a knife. Whatever else I was, I was not a depressive and had never exhibited suicidal tendencies. Violent? Yes, maybe, but only if provoked and even then more verbally than physically violent. Wasn't it healthier, anyway, to express my anger, rather than hold it in? With the case for brain surgery overruled, my mother decided to take the driving seat from then on; I would remain ill over her dead body.

The School Certificate

In the end, my mother decided to 'think outside the box' and she got my despairing father to agree that what I most needed was companionship – preferably outside the home. So a young man was sent from an agency to tutor me for the School Certificate in a rented London flat. This gentleman, a wartime Oxford graduate, was the very model of patience and Christian compassion.

Despite initial worries that our relationship would follow the usual pattern of blaming tantrums, I ended up rather liking him. He listened to what I said and I felt he wasn't a million miles from understanding me. But the sun of his empathy couldn't outshine the storm clouds. And he did have some irritating habits, like insisting I went to bed at a certain time. Things like that reminded me too much of school. I tried to persuade my parents to tell him off but, of course, they refused! By then, I'd become increasingly impatient with him.

After a series of blazing bust-ups, I decided to be a bit forceful and show him, once and for all, who was boss by tearing up his book of Common Entrance papers and notebooks which he used for teaching another pupil. Perhaps unsurprisingly, he wrote a letter to my parents, admitting defeat and tendering his resignation.

Switching prisms, now, from tormented teenager to adult, I'm happy to record that my mother later persuaded this kind gentleman to return and give me a spot more tutoring. We subsequently became lifelong friends and, at the age of ninety-three, he still knows his trigonometry from his quadratic equations.

A diamond of a man

One has to move on and my parents accordingly did. My mother then introduced me to the second most wonderful man I've ever met. Dr M., as I'll call him, was a retired family doctor of seventy-eight. I doubt he even knew what OCD was and, in my book at the time, that was a big plus. Unlike today, little was known about OCD sixty years ago and, anyway, it didn't matter since it was Dr M.'s humanity, not textbook knowledge, that was to rescue me from further regression.

I felt as if Dr M. treated me as his equal, and we talked adult-to-adult. He didn't treat me, as everybody else had, like some sick child incapable of recovery. He never once told me not to do anything; he kind of trusted me. In fact, I don't think OCD was even mentioned in our chats. Instead, he engaged me in other, more interesting, things and demonstrated to me, for example, how the mind can control the body. Incredibly, he showed me how, by just concentrating for three minutes, he could arrest the blood flow to his leg and make it go stone cold . . .

Steps towards cure

He got on very well with my mother, too, I noticed. I suddenly began seeing her more through his eyes and knew they both wanted the best for me. The atmosphere in the house somehow seemed to get much freer. My father shelled out £60 to buy me a pony from the local stables and I called him Rover. To my surprise, I was allowed to ride him wherever I wanted. I soon felt very close to Rover and told him some of my secrets; I was sure he understood.

Then, to my surprise and delight, I got given a 125cc Norman motorcycle for my birthday, which I'd ride down the path and around the front lawn in crazy mud-churning circles, revelling in my new-found freedom and sharing it with my new-found friend.

It was not that Dr M. had ever instructed me in so many words to get out of my bedroom, leave the house and reconnect with life. In his immense wisdom, he realized that it was the carrot, not the stick, that motivated me and my dear mother had the insight to act on his good advice and bring my father along with them.

Then, for some reason, my mother was anxious I should meet a 'lady friend' of hers in London. I wasn't too keen but, to please her, I agreed and we met for tea at my parents' London club. We actually travelled up by train, which, given my earlier incapacity, was quite an achievement for me. Her friend seemed pleasant enough and didn't talk down to me, which was refreshing – just warm acceptance and an encouraging smile.

Tea and crumpets

My mother said later how much her friend liked me. That made a change . . . Then, out of the blue, came a card from this lady, seeking my advice on learning French. Could I spare the time to meet her for tea at a teashop in Baker Street the following Friday? I didn't see why not. Since she needed my help, it would have been churlish to refuse. Besides, I knew that the food at Wizards was good. I expected my mother to stay with us, but she suddenly had some urgent shopping to do and left . . .

Despite butter being rationed, my mother's friend used her charm with the waiter to wrangle me some extra until my crumpets were swimming in it. I was well impressed. After helping her with her French, I told her what a terrible time I'd had coping with all those shrinks. She laughed. We got on like a house on fire and arranged another meeting. For some reason, she quickly lost interest in her French, but that didn't seem to matter now. Soon, I was well enough to take the train alone to see her in London.

Then, some months later, she invited me to her 'office' in Queen Anne Street. I thought it was odd that she would live in that area, linked as it was to the medical profession, but I supposed there must be some non-medical people with flats there. After sitting me down in the most comfortable armchair, she offered me a cup of tea and a couple of delicious fruit bars.

Blown cover

It slowly dawned on me that she was a shrink, a psychologist in a boys' school, with a couple of doctorates in medicine and theology! Had I known that on day one, I'd have fled the room but, now that I regarded her as a friend, it didn't seem to matter. A crucial and unbreakable bond of friendship was thus forged with this lady, which lasted for the rest of her life and most of mine. That friendship is testimony to the extraordinary care both my mother and this lady doctor took to manage my illness in its early stages. Without it, I would assuredly have drowned in the turbulent maelstrom of my OCD.

But, far from this being the end of my rescue, it was only the start. Despite my new-found saviour's formidable emotional intelligence, it was a few more years before I realized that I had broken free of OCD's python-like grip.

Indeed, the immediate, most critical, challenge was to prevent my having a second nervous breakdown as that would have done for me. Dr A., the lady psychologist, warned my parents that another breakdown would have been incurable

So how, against this stark reality, were my remaining teenage years to be micro-managed? In a letter to my parents, Dr A. wrote that my 'human need' for friendship and understanding were greater than the need for an academic education, with all its stresses on my nervous health.

The keynote problem

So bang went my formal education and any hope, it seemed, of ever getting to university. I felt that in the eyes of other boys, I would look even more stupid and ignorant than I already was.

However, in reality, Dr A. had written to a leading education consultant that she thought there was nothing intrinsically wrong with me, but that I used my high IQ to mock and upset people. What she omitted to mention was that putting people down made me feel superior and was balm to a badly bruised teenage ego. I hadn't the maturity, of course, to see it through her eyes as a problem. But it was good, nonetheless, having always thought myself stupid, to be told otherwise.

I did find it frustrating to communicate with other people, but only in the sense that it was sometimes hard work getting them to agree and act on my agenda and, in some instances, to 'unhook' me from my obsessional thoughts by answering my questions in a certain way. That was the problem as I then perceived it. I never attempted to develop a patient attitude as, on the contrary, I found *impatience* – genuine or not – often enabled me to get to the core of a matter. I now look back and see in my earlier self a thoroughly obnoxious teenager.

Unorthodox approach

Dr A. saw herself as fulfilling the role of an aunt who also happened to be a physician. She was thinking of inviting me down to her country cottage at weekends, where I would meet older colleagues who would provide intellectual stimulus. She would combine this with a one-to-one talk so that 'treatment' remained unobtrusive. She thought it best to carry on in this unorthodox fashion, which to me was the only tolerable way forward.

She saw me at the time as a very sick and bewildered individual in urgent need of a relationship where I couldn't ridicule people. Given the right kind of help, she predicted I could fulfil my full potential and, thankfully, she turned out to be right. So what constituted the right kind of help in an age that predated cognitive behaviour therapy and customized OCD medication? The answer lies in the way my teenage years were micro-managed by my mother and two remarkable carers.

Today's OCD specialists would, I think, be the first to acknowledge that, effective though CBT and medication are, they have proven even more effective when the patient's human needs are also met through the enlightened support of carers and loved ones. Since, apart from brain surgery, there was little else around in that immediate post-war period, I believe I was healed by *love*.

Just before her death, Dr A. handed me a large treasure-trove of correspondence between my parents, doctors, school heads, educationalists and, of course, myself; and it is from that archive that I've occasionally drawn for my story. It is clear that my indomitable parents had to kiss many frogs before coming up with their princess in Dr A. and their prince in Dr M. Unlike today, little was known about OCD in the late 1940s and my parents found it extremely frustrating trying to track down a treatment that was effective. In a letter written to my female psychiatrist, my father gives full vent to his past frustration and present bewilderment: 'With a boy so fundamentally normal, I can't understand why a majority of doctors gave up on him and why Dr. M. alone saw the life force in Robert, despite his utter lack of interest in life at the time, including even motor-cycling and cricket.'

A redemptive choice

I later read one of my father's letters saying that due to my doctors' advice, 'we reversed all the constraints to which we had previously subjected Robert and, in their place, gave him absolute freedom. This was in contrast to all our former ideas and we have learnt our lesson.' Such self-abasing humility on my father's part I find quite breathtaking. For the first time I understood the personal sacrifice he made for me and could hate him no longer.

It was my parents' and doctors' love and compassion, and their naked faith in my powers of recovery, that saved my life. Both my doctors – however unorthodox their methods – were trained physicians, but they were also gifted with a rare degree of emotional intelligence and were able to get inside my psyche and heal me from within. So my belated thanks to you, Dad, for trusting my mother's intuition in these matters and allowing my twin lifebelts to hold my head above the water through all my stormy tantrums.

Since we know that one size does not fit all, there is a strong case for trying on every shoe in the shop – as my parents did – until we get a proper fit! It is very good to learn from the range of other people's experiences, and hopefully this book will help to show that they are several ways forward towards recovery.

I have been involved in facilitating OCD groups, seminars and workshops, but all too often, if the facilitator allows, the focus of these groups is on symptoms rather than on solutions leading to recovery. I was fortunate that my mother and my father stopped worrying about my symptoms, my panic and tactlessness, because they knew that they would pass with my recovery.

Keeping the faith

It is only now, in writing this, that I've come to realize that it was the sustaining love of my parents that put me, like Humpty Dumpty, back together again.

My dear sister – who has been hugely supportive of me throughout my adult life – was then too young to know what was going on and was, in any case, away at school most of the time. Because my parents remained in denial during the first phase of my illness, they never told her that I was ill, merely that I was 'a bit odd'. She, of course, agreed since, when at home from school, she had to be part of my support network.

What strikes me as important in this family context is not that I was brought up in a nuclear family, but that I was brought up by two people who loved each other, thus demonstrating to the children, however subliminally, *how* to love. I don't believe that my two physicians alone, however visionary, could have rescued me without the bedrock of my mother's unconditional love. It was the happy combination of both that proved to be the magic formula.

Dogs and children

Not a single snap in the family album shows my father touching either me or my sister. With his children at least, he wasn't just non-tactile, he was *anti*-tactile. Dogs were different; Bruce and Trixie were forever in evidence on his lap, being stroked and played with. But, when our mother gave us babies the same attention, she was reproved for spoiling us – and she duly desisted for thirteen love-starved years.

However, once our parents finally had a change of heart and began to demonstrate their affection for their pathetically ill son, it was catch-up time and my mother, guided as ever by Dr M. and Dr A. – at long last felt free to show how much she loved me. And that, combined with Rover and my new-found freedom, was like fresh water to a dying plant; my spirits rose and my interest in life slowly began to return. My OCD was finally about to be seriously challenged . . .

One more misjudgement in my treatment could have resulted in a pre-frontal leucotomy, sectioning to a mental institution or even suicide. An exchange of letters in the spring and summer of 1949 may give some idea of the new game plan that would either make or break me.

A chronic illness?

First came Dr A.'s acute analysis of the problem. In a letter to Dr M., dated 5 March 1949, she wrote that, when people didn't come up to my expectations, I'd become difficult and resentful, using my high IQ and intuition in a negative and aggressive way. This led me to end up in a discouraged, tense state which tended to aggravate the obsessional tendency. She was worried that the resultant stress could then develop into a chronic illness. She would need to keep a close watch on it.

Then, six weeks later, on 20 April, my mother wrote that she felt partly responsible for starting my OCD in the first place: 'The boy's illness was caused by the lack of sufficient physical and mental stimulation since early babyhood. Repression and scolding and lack of encouragement at home and prep. school have, I'm sure, caused his lack of confidence in us and himself.' She said that if she and my father had believed everything they were told in various reports about my behaviour, I would never have been cured: 'we have now finally come to understand the boy' and were determined not to send me to an institution, thanks to 'Dr. M.'s unshakeable faith in R's potential for recovery'.

What, after sixty-one years, I find so moving in this narrative is the unflinching and unsparing way my parents faced up to their past shortcomings; their later objectivity was not clouded by a single iota of fudging, self-deception or denial. Without her tigerish tenacity and intuitive grasp of my needs and potential, my mother could never have steered her way unscathed through a veritable minefield of conflicting medical and, as we shall see, educational recommendations. My parents could not have done more to atone for past mistakes.

But OCD, alas, has to be fought every inch of the way. The aim was not merely to alleviate my symptoms; to quieten me down; to have me function in a sheltered environment and to accept that, during the course of my life, there would inevitably be periods of regression. No, that was not my mother's purpose at all. Her non-negotiable objective – without the benefit of modern treatments – was nothing less than to have me make a complete recovery without a single regressive lapse and to have a happy and successful career in direct competition with my peers.

Battles to come

In the battles that followed, neither my mother nor I could afford to lose; we would swim or drown together. As, at this point (early March 1949), my parents were still not entirely singing from the same hymn sheet, progress still marched with a limp. 'Robert's father,' wrote Dr A. to another doctor on 5 March 1949, 'wishes to consult Dr. P. regarding their boy. The husband and wife, I think, are still apt to pull in opposite ways over the lad's treatment and I shall be very glad if Dr. P. can act here in the role of Solomon!'

So what form would my treatment take? Dr A. was glad to have Dr P.'s endorsement of her own take on the matter, which was that an analytic approach would be unsuitable and that, 'Probably, the only feasible course is some mild psychotherapy in the way of helping and directing, very tactfully applied.'

A happy component of this 'mild psychotherapy' were weekend visits to her country cottage. 'Over last weekend at the cottage,' she wrote to Dr P. on 19 April 1949, 'Robert mixed very well and appears happy and almost symptom-free. He is also rapidly making friends with boys of his own age and I think will manage now with carefully-spaced psycho-therapeutic help.'

Cricket rules, OK?

It was on the strength of this seemingly rapid improvement that I was sent to another private boarding school – or, rather, to some local landlady's boarding house as I wasn't yet considered capable of sharing a school house with a crowd of other boys.

Given the general medical consensus that any undue academic pressure was out, a battle royal ensued between my mother and the school head to ensure that it stayed out.

On this pivotal issue, the school head and the school psychologist pulled in an opposite direction to my mother who, as always, had to hold her ground.

Because my hitherto all-pervasive OCD had locked me into my unremitting 24/7 search for relief – and indeed survival – it had drowned out all outside interests, which meant that school curriculum subjects held not the slightest interest for me. Teach a child something that interests him and he will be energized, but teach him something that bores him and he will be stressed, and stress was something that I had to avoid at all costs.

I had at least improved sufficiently by then for cricket to resume its place as my one abiding passion and my mother immediately grasped how much it could contribute to my recovery.

With a sliver of Thatcherite steel in her pen, my mother wrote to Dr A. on 20 May that: 'I simply don't hold with the school psychologist's view that Robert is skiving and that what he needs is more intensive study . . . his education must not come at the cost of another breakdown . . . Play, not work, is indeed his cure.' She believed that the first priority was to make up for my repressed, pleasure-starved early years and that cricket was part of the remedy.

Too much to bear

But could all this have come too late? Behind those cricket stumps, the OCD was again rearing its ugly head. My mother wrote a distressed letter to Dr A. on 3 July, saying that I was 'overwhelmed with the feeling that everything was just too much to bear'. She had spoken to the relative of a brain specialist who warned her that, 'OCD is a quagmire, so don't be too optimistic about your son's recovery'. As a result, she was still concerned that my nervous system would not stand up to life later on. She wanted to make sure that some sort of progress was being made and that I would be able to live with other human beings.

My parents were not allowed much contact with the school, so Dr A. wrote to the headmaster: 'I should appreciate having a brief confidential report on Robert's conduct at school. Seen from my end, he behaves like a poisonous brat, but there is no doubt that his obsessional symptoms are still there to a slight degree and no risk must be taken that these flare up again as I doubt if he would recover a second time. As I see it, the two great risks in his life are a too vivid realization of his present unpleasant self and being too pushed with study.'

The headmaster's report was a stinker, and claimed that aspirin consumption in my digs had gone up considerably since my arrival. As for my landlady's report, she was too apoplectic to write anything beyond: 'Impossible to make a report on this difficult character; he was arrogant and selfish to the utmost.'

A fortnight later, Dr A. wrote that 'when the lad comes to my cottage at weekends, no obsessive, only infantile, behaviour is observable. He behaves like a perfectly normal, very intelligent, likeable and spoilt boy. As he has improved almost unbelievably, he cannot do better, in my view, than remain in his present school.' However, I wasn't able to make the move from the landlady's house into a school house as none of the housemasters were willing to try to cope with me. It came as quite a stunner to my parents when I offered my own solution, blithely volunteering to return for a final year to my original public school. Faced by their incredulity, I pushed the cricket and that swung it.

My mother's death

As my new, and most amiable, housemaster did not believe in the birch, I spent a final year in my old house. I was sat at the top of the seniors table with my age group, but every meal was torture as I suffered from blushing problems, stemming from my deep sense of inadequacy. However, I did, belatedly, sit my School Certificate at the ripe old age of seventeen and also played cricket for the college second eleven.

That autumn of 1951 I hitch-hiked my way to Austria, where I enrolled for a year at university and, after a few months, was writing home to my mother in German. Although I couldn't play cricket there, I did learn to ski. In 1952, I crossed the Brenner Pass and enrolled for a second year in an Italian university, whilst happily living with an Italian family.

Whilst studying abroad, my mother contracted breast cancer. When home during that period, I helped to nurse her. During that Christmas of 1952 – the worst of my life – she couldn't eat and was nothing but skin-and-bones, with a large open ulcer on her scalp. Her death, in the first week of 1953, was the worst shock of my entire life and I've never fully recovered from it. How can you recover from the loss of someone to whom you owe your happiness and very survival?

Despite the physical ravages, which she gave every sign of ignoring, my mother's was a happy death. In willing me through my illness, she had succeeded against all the odds in setting her son on the road to health and happiness. Had she invested less in me, imagine the distress she would have felt in having failed in her mission. I bless her memory and, after fifty-eight years, still feel just as close to her as ever My father, in the meantime, was languishing in an upstairs bedroom, with his right side and arm paralysed from a recent stroke. His death, within hours of my mother's, struck my seventeen-year-old sister particularly hard as she was once closer to him than I.

A place at Cambridge

I returned to my studies, which I found difficult as I was still scared of 'losing' myself in a book. None the less, after a few months' private tuition, I got my O level in Latin, which, in those days, was a prerequisite for entry to Oxbridge. I soon followed this with four A levels and, after a successful interview, I secured a place at Cambridge University. This seemed to me at the time to be a quite normal thing for me to do. If, however, Dr A. and my mother had not wisely withheld from me how critically ill I had been, I would not have had the bottle to apply there for a place!

I'd like to think that this part of my story has less to do with symptoms (the problem) than with goals and aspiration (the solution); that, in transcending our symptoms, we also help to neutralize them. In my journey towards recovery, I found to my delight that there are other, more holistic, signs of recovery than the mere absence of symptoms.

OCD is far from being the only battle I've had to fight – and win – in my life and I've found that work on one's self-image is another potent way of relieving symptoms. I believe there is a whole raft of things we can do for ourselves to build on and maximize the help we receive from specialists.

National Service

It didn't occur to me that I could apply for, and be granted, exemption from doing my National Service on medical grounds. As a skier, squash and tennis player, I felt perfectly capable of fighting for Queen and country. Besides, my Cambridge place had been deferred until after my military service. Ironically, the main obstacle to my joining up was Dr A. since she was convinced at the time that I would never hack it. But the only way she could deter me from joining up was by coming clean over the seriousness of my illness, the very thing she was trying to keep from me. So, rather than tell me, she took other measures.

She fired her first shot at the Ministry of Labour's Chief Allocation Officer, a full nine months before I would even be old enough, at eighteen, to join up! She said that I would break down severely and irreversibly under the strain of military training and that my OCD would then be likely to remain with me for the rest of my life. The Ministry seemed distinctly underwhelmed by those early pleas for exemption. This was understandable because at that time many perfectly healthy young men, seeking exemption, were professing some form of mental or physical disability.

But Dr A. persevered and wrote to the Ministry in September 1951, expressing her dismay that they should find it necessary to summon me to appear before their Medical Board. I had recently suffered, she wrote reprovingly, a most grave mental illness in the form of a particularly florid obsessional neurosis which had crippled me. Moreover, neither my parents nor I had ever been allowed to realize how very ill I was. I'd been seen by many eminent psychiatrists, she continued, and the prognosis was considered so bad that a pre-frontal leucotomy had been recommended. Besides, she concluded, I would be of no use to the Services, only an expense.

Amazingly, the Ministry still demanded to see me in person. Then, for some unknown reason, the Board became intent on *dissuading* me from enlisting. In my naivety and ignorance, I thought it was my myopia that was the problem, but I think I persuaded them that, if I could see to drive my sports car, I could also see well enough to shoot the enemy. Anyway, I finally got the Board to agree to take me and I duly joined the Intelligence Corps. After a year's intensive Russian course, I became an accredited Home Office interpreter. Dr A. never told me of her strenuous behind-the-scenes campaign to get me exempted and I only learnt about it from the personal archive she left me on her death.

Good results

On 24 August 1955 my medical guardian angel, Dr A., wrote to Brigadier D., asking that, at my Medical Board demobilization, no reference be made to my previous mental history. She thought that the kindest act might be simply to congratulate me on my academic results whilst serving in the Royal Air Force. And that is exactly what, in their wisdom, the Board did. Officially, at least, my OCD was dead and buried. No one could have been happier to be proved wrong than Dr A. Despite her well-founded fears, I had *not* broken down under the strain of being a national serviceman – partly because I continued seeing her in London and partly because, in mastering a very difficult new language, I was able to do something I loved. For the first time in my life, I was excelling at something and, within that holistic context, the OCD symptoms took care of themselves.

As well as finding out that I was able to work hard, the new-found respect of my peers did wonders for my self-esteem and enabled me to go from strength to strength. Treatment of OCD by the professionals is, of course, by far the best tool but, for optimum results, it needs to be part of a wider toolset. Another factor was the sheer sense of liberation I felt, freed at long last from the semi-obsessive reach of my father and the suffocating discipline he imposed on my childhood. There was a surprising amount of freedom in the Forces, which was further indulged at Cambridge and was the making of my recovery.

My recovery seems, even to me now, remarkable – and humbling – in the light of the unanimous recommendation of Dr G. and colleagues that I undergo brain surgery because of the risk of suicide later. Even the ever-watchful Dr A., whilst not agreeing with them, did warn my GP as late as July 1965 that, as those doctors were analytically and not physically minded, their views needed to be taken very seriously.

OCD's long shadow

Studying with the Forces should, arguably, have prepared me for student life. It didn't. OCD, I discovered, casts a very long shadow. I might have been pretty much symptom-free, but that didn't mean that I was anywhere near being as socially and emotionally functional as I would have been had I never had OCD.

I remember my hands actually trembling when I offered glasses of sherry to my fellow student lodgers in my first-year digs. I'd never given a party before in my life; for me, that was as scary as one's first parachute jump. My self-esteem, after its initial boost, was still in bud.

But, in my final two undergraduate years, it blossomed. I found the university's social, intellectual and physical freedom quite intoxicating and my time there was the making of me. In addition to getting a good degree, I learned a second Slav language and even won a European scholarship.

After a spell in the Foreign Office and in academia, much of my working life has been spent as a freelance feature writer for the national broadsheets, along with some broadcasting and public speaking. The golden thread throughout my life so far has been words. My first stage play had a professional London production and features a creatively gifted youth who develops OCD, as a direct result of being hog-tied to his authoritarian father's wish to clone him.

Life after OCD

I consider my life to be much sweeter for having lived in a form of prison during what should have been a highly creative period of my life – my teenage years. Once freed from my OCD, I felt propelled like a rocket by all that long-suppressed adolescent energy, which still propels me on the same trajectory. It must be like having your cataracts removed – all the colours around you suddenly become so much richer, so much more vibrant.

And the people you meet suddenly become so much more interesting: their clothes, their body language, their quirkiness. And you become greedy, ravenous even, for knowledge; with every subject awaiting your interest and questions. You look forward to getting up in the morning. You may say I'd feel like this anyway, even without the OCD. I doubt that very much. I will never retire; I did retirement as a teenager.

Regression-proof?

The evidence that my OCD was in the past came in 1999 when I accidentally ran into an oncoming black cab and shattered my left temple, which had to be reconstructed. In my OCD days, it would have taken much less than that to send me into a long tailspin, attempting to undo the accident by endlessly repeated obsessive thinking. The rational side of me knew that the accident was entirely my own fault but reason is a stranger to OCD. The point is that, previously, my OCD side just could not accept reality. As it could not undo the physical fact of the accident, the only 'logical' course left would be to undo it in my head by ritual thinking. Pain of obsessive thinking for me was less than the pain of living with an even more painful reality.

My sister and I both agreed that if anything could have triggered my OCD, this accident would have done. It didn't. Indeed, it didn't even occur to me to call on OCD for some 'magical' solution to my problems. My former illness had passed the ultimate litmus test and I felt – and still feel – that I was no longer in danger of relapsing.

Facing reality

In retrospect, I'm not sure whether my father's repression really was the cause or the trigger of my OCD as I think it was probably latent in me, possibly from birth. I'm not sure now that one needs to identify the root cause of a sufferer's OCD other than in the most general terms in order to eradicate it. What I do know helped me enormously was the overnight change of environment – the oxygen of freedom: the pony, the motorcycle, the sudden absence of constraints and discipline, the blank cheque to go and do what I pretty well liked. I found that whole heady cocktail utterly intoxicating as I was finally allowed to live the reality of being me.

Sad to relate, OCD has a long shadow that stretches way past the immediate removal of symptoms. I may have been cured at the symptom level, but it took me years to make good the collateral damage of my 'lost' childhood. I would never have been able to start the journey, though, without the wonderful emotional launch pad of my mother and Dr A. Those two women were able to love and accept me because they understood me.

It's hard to love and accept someone if you don't understand them – and OCD is very hard to understand. And who better to explain OCD to the sufferer's loved ones than the professionals? Without Dr A.'s sensitive guidance, my mother could not have directed her love to such good effect.

Never a victim!

OCD doctors are best placed, for instance, to explore with families and partners how far they can safely go along with a sufferer's rituals and obsessions. Dr A. warned my mother against being too compliant and going along too far with my OCD behaviour. Far from helping me, Dr A. told her she risked tipping me over into the 'poor me' victim role which can infantilize the sufferer and render him that much less able to help himself. My mother felt very torn, as it went against the grain for her to draw up, and stick to, strict boundaries.

I feel I was many things in my journey out of OCD, but I was never a passive victim. Had I not been very proactive in getting my mother to deal with my father, I doubt she would ever have brought him round to allowing me the freedom he did. Anger, of course, is not a long-term solution, but it is important to be assertive and communicate one's needs and I feel it is infinitely preferable to passive victimhood.

Physical health

I believe my sustained recovery owes as much to my physical as to my mental health. It's very hard to remain stressed after a good hard swim! And stress is OCD's best friend; it positively feasts on stress.

I'm convinced that a month spent in my late teens at an Outward Bound sea school in Wales, involving sailing and long hill treks, contributed significantly to my recovery. It provided me with an insight into the holistic value of physical fitness that set me on a lifelong course of daily exercise involving weekly swimming and Hatha yoga which I have found to be hugely beneficial. Indeed, I see regular exercise as a free insurance premium against illness.

Positive thinking

Coupled with the huge enjoyment of life that comes from keeping physically and mentally fit, the final item in my toolset is positive thinking, which I've practised ever since Dr M. demonstrated to me the power of our minds.

I've left this strategy until last as I see it as OCD's worst enemy. It finds positive thinkers highly indigestible and spits them out in disgust. I never get out of bed in the morning without first thinking of five good things that either happened to me yesterday or that I'm looking forward to today.

It's hard, if you do that, to feel bad for long. If you try to fight the dark thoughts on their own ground, you're attaching too much importance to them. After all, if you're in a dark room, you don't try to fight the darkness; you simply switch on the light and the darkness disappears. After a while, I found this habit of positive thinking came quite naturally to me. It makes you friends, too!

And, whatever you do, don't bear grudges or harbour resentments; it's very depleting. I personally find myself incapable of bearing a grudge for more than about two minutes as it's too much like hard work. Surrounded by all these enemies, OCD will eventually give up on you and move on to softer targets. Believe me, I know.

Conclusion

What worked – and still works – for me may well not work for you. All I can do here is show you the route map that led me from the depths of a crippling illness to full recovery and a happy life. You can do it; it can be done!

Concepts are more important than detail; don't allow yourself to get too bogged down with your symptoms. Try, in your clearer moments, to think *outside* the box. Trust me, it works.

The one simple lesson I draw from my earlier roller-coaster of a journey is that a proactively holistic approach is best suited to defeating OCD. A passive, unquestioning 'if you say so, doctor' response to treatment is, I believe, likely to produce a poor prognosis. The most that even your therapist can offer you is a route map to recovery, but it's *you* who have to walk it!

Form a good working partnership with your OCD specialist. Ask them questions and act on their advice as I did with Dr A. and Dr M. Do the CBT or other homework they set you. If you see your doctor as a gym instructor, remember it's you who have to do the workouts!

To maximize the value of therapy and medication, I believe we could do a lot worse than live healthily, think positively, actively search out the sunbeams among the clouds and, above all, enjoy the rewards that will come from such an approach. Hoist yourself above the cloud-banks and let the world be your oyster. The view from the top of Everest is sensational!

9

Not plain sailing

My GP's consulting room was quiet. I was sitting opposite him and he was looking intently but with concern at me. I had started to tell him of my problems when he suddenly picked up the phone and rang through to reception. He requested that he was to have no interruptions from anyone for the time being. Meanwhile I sat there feeling utterly miserable. I still don't know how I managed to tell him how awful my thoughts were. I was so ashamed of them as they were not a true representation of my character. Yet to this day, I am so glad I did. That half-hour with him changed my life!

Perhaps I had better start at the beginning because this appointment had been a long time in coming. It is now nearly eighteen years since I told my GP – I was then forty-three. I cannot say exactly when my OCD started but I do know that as a child and teenager I was a dreadful worrier! I didn't know that random thoughts are natural. I honestly believed that they were God's way of tempting me. As I got older my thoughts began to revolve around the idea of hurting someone. My mother was a teacher and I remember going into her school and being concerned that I might inadvertently lock a child in a cupboard. Of course, I never did. Later, when I was at teacher training college I became very concerned about the kettles in the corridors of the residential halls. Health and safety was not a big issue then and so kettles could often be found steaming away on the corridor floor.

I had finished training as a teacher and was in my first appointment at a primary school in Durham, when my OCD reared its ugly head. I was twenty-three years old and I had gone home for Christmas. I knew that my father was ill but as I had been told that he had sclerosis of the liver I had hoped to see an improvement in him. Instead I found that his bed had been moved downstairs and he looked very ill indeed. I remember going into the kitchen and saying to my mother that I was really worried about him. It was then that she decided to tell me the truth – he had cancer of the liver and pancreas. For the last two or three months my mother had been carrying the burden of the true nature of my father's illness by herself, along with one or two close friends. She had even told my father that he had sclerosis of the liver, as she wanted him to have hope. I was shocked and felt guilty because only a few months earlier, before he had any diagnosis, I had jokingly stated that it might be cancer, never really thinking that it might be. I felt awful for him and hated to see him struggling and looking so ill.

Three days later, I returned to Durham to start the Spring term. As soon as I possibly could, I went to see my headmaster and told him that I could be summoned home at any time, probably in the next fortnight or so, as my father was desperately ill. I remember that day so well. Before I had left my parent's house, I had been in the kitchen and seen a cut glass which my father had been given for Christmas. Then I had seen some bottles of household cleaner in the cupboard under the kitchen sink. Travelling back to Durham by train I remember congratulating myself that I hadn't put anything in the glass, which could hurt my father. I was not going to be bothered by that thought or so I believed! In assembly that first morning back at school I prayed that God should take my father and he should not suffer anymore. Just after lunch, the headmaster came into my room and told me that my father, who was only sixty, had passed away. My brother was coming to fetch me.

It was such a shock that I suppose in some ways I feel it was almost inevitable that my OCD would cause me so much trouble in the years to come. After all, I'd had the thought of maybe putting something into his glass to poison him in order to end his pain, and I had prayed so earnestly that his suffering should finish. I just had not expected him to die so soon. My mind would not now accept that I had not put anything into his glass. I was overwhelmed with the thought that he had died because of me. My mother, many years later, told me that several people had felt that they were responsible in some way for my father getting cancer or even dying. The next few years were a living hell. I continued to teach but marking books took longer than it should have done because I was continually going back over them to check that I hadn't written any comment about killing my father. If I wrote a letter to someone, I would often have to open the envelope and check that I hadn't written anything about my father's death. The envelope would be sealed and have a stamp on it but I would still open it. Sometimes, I would have reached the post box only to have to return home, open the envelope and check it again. Not only did I feel so guilty about my father's death but at this time I also lived in fear – of being found guilty and sent to prison. All this time I never told anyone of my thoughts. Furthermore, I had no idea that there was a condition called OCD.

During this time, I married and eventually had a son. Towards the beginning of my marriage I tried to explain to my husband what was happening to me but I felt that he really didn't want to know and couldn't understand it. I never tried again and so I continued living a very troubled life. As I started to believe that I had not killed my father, my OCD 'mutated'. Now, the slightest thought that I might hurt somebody in any way would set me off checking, checking and checking that I hadn't hurt that person. When I was expecting my son I had the sudden thought of taking a painkiller and, even though I didn't take it, I spent the next seven months worrying about the fact that I might have hurt my unborn child. In fact, when he was born, he was totally healthy and I was so relieved. There was nothing wrong with him! The next five years were probably the best five years of my life. I really enjoyed seeing him grow up and reach the age of five. I still had to contend with my OCD but it had calmed down and become manageable. I was fortunate in that my husband took on extra work to provide us with a higher income and so I only did the very occasional day's supply teaching.

However, when my son started infant school my husband persuaded me to apply for a part-time teaching post at a school which he had heard was a good one. Unfortunately, over the last few years it had changed and now had many difficult pupils in it. Once I started working there my stress levels rose and my negative thoughts became far more intrusive. So I had learned that my OCD waxed and waned with my levels of stress. During the five years that I was at home with my son I'd had some difficulty with cooking meals for the family but it was all very manageable. Now that I was teaching again in a stressful situation and also trying to keep my family going, I started to have even more problems with cooking. I would prepare the vegetables, rinse them and then keep rinsing them! When I eventually got them on the hob, I would sometimes feel the need to take them off again and start rinsing them again. Had I put something in them that would hurt either my husband or my son? Of course not, but my brain would not accept that. My fear of hurting others began to impinge upon other areas of my life as well. Going to the theatre, a love of mine, started to become difficult. I would settle down to watch a play and then suddenly I would have the thought that I might have hurt the person in front of me. So I would have to look at them to see if they were all right; back to the play, check again, back to the play, check again and this would continue throughout the performance. The same would happen at the cinema. There is little pleasure to be gained from going to the theatre or cinema when your mind will not settle!

Then I started to become scared of any electrical item being near water. For some time now I'd had difficulty in believing that I had turned off any tap I'd used. Overflowing water could cause damage and even cause electrical problems – or so I thought. I might have put the plug into water and then the next person to use the electrical item could die! Puff – he could go up in a cloud of smoke! These thoughts really did impinge upon my life and to some extent still do. It was fortunate that we discovered that the wiring in our home was unsafe – the electric wires were sheathed in rubber, which had deteriorated. One day we found, to our horror, that the electrical socket in our son's bedroom had nearly caused a fire. The house was rewired. Out went the old-fashioned fuse-box and in came a unit which contained circuit breakers. So, without anyone knowing, I had got rid of that worry in my house because if there was a fault with an appliance the circuit breaker would trip. This enabled me to relax far more at home. When eventually we did move house, the first thing I asked for was a circuit breaker to be installed. Fortunately my husband agreed.

During this time, I learnt to drive and eventually passed my test. However, this was not a success. If I passed a cyclist on the road I would immediately have the thought that I might have knocked him off his cycle and perhaps even killed him. If my husband was with me I felt more secure and I could cope. When I drove by myself I felt I had to keep checking and checking in the mirror that all was well with whoever I might have passed. I realized that by checking in the mirror I could be becoming a danger to the traffic in front of me. For this reason, I gave up driving by myself. Fortunately we only had one car and so it did not become too much of an issue with my husband. When my marriage eventually broke up, I became and still am reliant on public transport. I have not driven now for over seventeen years.

Holidays too became a nightmare. If we stayed at a hotel my mind would immediately search out any electrical item – I had no control over this habit of searching for danger. In my mind's eye, a hairdryer could be immersed in water; similarly a kettle might be moved and immersed in water or the water it contained could be poured over an electric plug. So I was very relieved when my husband, who loved holidays, decided that it would be a good idea to get a caravan. We could connect it to the site's main electricity supply and I left that to him. However, because we didn't have a new caravan with its own plumbing, we still had to use the site's own toilet facilities. So, unbeknown to my husband, our holidays became far less stressful for me because the only time I had to worry about electricity and water was if I saw a communal hairdryer anywhere near a tap in the shower block.

As you can see, unfortunately my OCD is not 'static'. Underlying it is the worry that I might cause harm to someone. There are lots of novels which contain a murder or two and I am sure you can think of many ways in which you could hurt someone. For most people, these thoughts will disappear in minutes if not seconds but that's not the case for me! Once I have had that kind of thought, I don't trust myself that I haven't committed that sin and so I have to keep checking that the 'victim' is still alive and well. My brain is very adept at thinking up numerous ways of hurting someone. I seem to have no control over it – I can assure you that I do not want those thoughts! For example, if I see a child crossing a bridge, I might have the thought that I could push him off it. I would then immediately have to start checking and checking again that he was still walking over the bridge or beyond. If I were to cross over that bridge another time, the same thoughts would occur to me and I'd have to keep checking again that I hadn't pushed someone off the bridge. It is such a horrible feeling being so unsure of oneself. I felt it was even more shameful because I am not like that – I hate to see anyone upset and/or hurting.

You might wonder how I coped with teaching. One great advantage of teaching is that you are so focused on teaching the pupils that your cares and worries tend to fade away. In my own classroom all was well. I won't deny that on one occasion, when I moved to a classroom which had a sink in it and I had to use an electrical appliance in that room, it did cause me some worry. Soon, though, the sink was removed and I was able to relax more. I did, however, hate doing cover lessons in science laboratories or cookery rooms. These were stressful in three ways; firstly, I often did not know the children and that could cause anxiety problems; secondly, as you can imagine, there were quite a lot of sinks and electrical items in these kinds of rooms; and thirdly there was the additional hazard of gas. I worried continually that the gas would accidentally be left on: one spark and the school would blow up! When I first started teaching at my last school our office had a kettle in it and much to my consternation, it was kept on the floor! It could, or so I thought, be left on and cause a fire hazard. When a computer was installed it gave me even more to worry about! I worried continually that I might pour water from the kettle on to it! The end of term always proved difficult for me because I could not go back and check that everything was safe. If anyone saw me they would wonder why I was there and I didn't want anyone to know my secret. However, I coped and when I retired from teaching I still had not told any of my colleagues about my anxious thoughts. There were several reasons for this. I felt very ashamed of my thoughts but I also didn't want people thinking that they had to treat me any differently or indeed if anything should happen that I should be the scapegoat. And, of course, I certainly didn't want the children to know.

People with OCD tend to be very adept at hiding their thoughts and movements from others. This was particularly true with me. However, I couldn't hide myself completely from my GP. It is not surprising that I suffered from depression and stress throughout those years. For some time I had regularly been going to see the same GP – each time he would try to get me to open up and each time I could not admit what was happening to me. I had seen other GPs in the past who just prescribed antidepressants but they never probed like this one did. For some unknown reason, I felt drawn to keep going back to him and when I saw him on that fateful day eighteen years ago, I had no idea that I was going to spill the beans. On reflection, I think I had just got to the point where I felt so desperately unhappy that the final push from my GP produced the result that he was waiting for. I cannot remember exactly what I told him but I do remember him sitting there patiently and intently, while listening to everything I said. He showed great concern and, more to the point, didn't condemn me! I was so ashamed of my thoughts that I didn't expect that. I definitely didn't expect him to say at the end that he could get some help for me. I thought nothing could be done except more antidepressants. He explained that I had a mental illness known as obsessive compulsive disorder. That was news to me. I had never heard of the illness before. He then told me that he had a friend, Ian, who was a clinical psychologist and he was sure that Ian would be able to help me. He would write to him. I remember leaving his room half-an-hour later with a prescription for an antidepressant, which he felt might well help me with my thoughts, and feeling utterly bewildered; I couldn't believe that I had actually told somebody about my thoughts. My mind was in turmoil – it felt like such a big step to have taken!

I didn't get an appointment straightaway and during this time I continued to worry – what had I done?!! Eventually, I saw the psychologist. I could hardly look at him. Of course, he asked me lots of questions, two of which I can remember. Firstly, he asked somewhat incredulously, 'Did you really tell no one over all those years?' The second question was to ask if I could work with him. He seemed such a kind, gentle man and, besides, I hadn't come this far to turn down an offer for help. I wanted to be able to enjoy life. As his diary was busy, I had to wait a few more weeks until we could have some regular sessions. Unfortunately, he had a lot of work to do with me – not just my OCD but also my depression. One of the first aspects of the treatment was to deal with my feelings of shame, intense self-criticism and dislike of myself. He tells me that he is still working on this but I have made a lot of progress! Writing this story shows me how far I have come. I am now happy to admit to people that I have OCD although I don't tend to admit how it affects me. This barrier is slowly being broken. I think it is because I have now retired from teaching and feel I have nothing to prove or lose.

One of the first conversations Ian had with me was to tell me that lots of people are afflicted with this illness. I couldn't believe it when he told me that there are surgeons who have OCD. 'But you can't open a body up again to check it!' I commented with some alarm. He then told me that people with OCD do not do the things that they are so frightened of doing. They are usually very careful and conscientious people. I certainly fitted into that category. Throughout my teaching career I never walked into a lesson without preparing it in advance. I took great care with marking children's work and with writing their reports.

We didn't get round to working with my electricity and water for a while. In the meantime my medication had been changed to an SSRI (selective serotonin reuptake inhibitor), which helped my depression and stopped me thinking over my problems so much. Ian felt that he needed to work on my shame, low self-esteem and depression. He also wanted me to understand OCD better. He showed me that my OCD was a bully and that I had to learn how to manage this bully! I needed to find ways to not act on what the bully was saying and to try to ignore it because, for example, the more I responded to what the bully demanded and checked and double-checked things, the more it would bully me into checking even more.

Eventually, part of my time with him involved confronting electrical appliances and water. I had told him that whenever I was away from home and saw an electrical appliance near a source of water, I would get very anxious and then I would feel a great need to check that all was well once I had left the room. So, part of the treatment was to spend some time in the ladies toilets where the cleaners left their hoovers. He told me to try not to fight the anxiety – easier said than done! Once I had left the toilets, I wasn't allowed to go back in and check that the water wasn't getting into the appliances. In fact, hard as it was, I didn't want to go back and check as that would mean that my OCD was winning. How long I stayed and what I did in the ladies varied. Sometimes I used the facilities and at other times I would fill the washbowl with water. I was always very aware that there were electrical items in very close proximity.

When Ian's place of work changed we were able to use the kitchen for this 'exposure' work. So I progressed to making Ian and myself a cup of tea in the kitchen shortly after my arrival. This task wasn't easy for me because there was an electric cooker next to the kitchen sink. There was also a toaster on the work surface. On some occasions, when I saw Ian in his consulting room, I was so determined to come to terms with my problems that I even voluntarily washed up whilst I was there. I would also practise leaving the room and not returning. In his consulting room he would ask how I felt and, if necessary, we would work on reducing my anxiety. I will never forget the time when Ian and I went into the kitchen and he deliberately flicked water at an electrical plug! He wanted to show me that nothing awful would happen but I was horrified and rapidly moved away! I even surprised myself at how violent my reaction was. Ian had to be quite firm with me to move back to his side. My appointment with Ian was often last thing in the afternoon and he would not be returning to that room for a few days. On these occasions he would often give me a large bottle to go to the kitchen to fill with water and then return to water his plants. I must admit I did not like the thought of watering the plant that was on a shelf above his computer. I was thankful that I wasn't tall enough!

Going on holiday is sometimes very difficult for me. When my marriage broke down I thought I might never go away again but in fact I did. I had a couple of holidays with my mother and stepfather in Wales. These weren't easy because I still had not told my mother about the nature of my OCD. So I decided that I needed to go away by myself. One of my hobbies is art and so I looked for an adult education class. In August 1999 I travelled to a residential adult education college. I knew that there would be water and electricity in the art room but I was determined to go. Of course, it wasn't easy, especially when I saw the sink in my bedroom, but I coped. I have kept the work I did with our tutor, Mr M., because I liked his fun style of painting and also because I was proud of my achievement of going on holiday. The following year I spent Easter at the same centre. Both holidays were difficult but I coped. In the first I had a washbowl in my bedroom and in the second a bath, washbowl and toilet. Fortunately, the only possible electrical item that I could damage was a bedside light. Nevertheless, it did interfere with my sleep and I must confess that it was not easy to leave my room at the end of the holidays because I wanted to go back and check that everything was safe.

The treatment I have received from Ian, over the years, has been a mixture of cognitive behaviour therapy and exposure. I hadn't been seeing Ian for long when he started to use cards on which he wrote new beliefs about my OCD for me to try to believe in. On the first card was:

> IT'S NOT ME
> IT'S MY OCD

On the reverse of this card is:

> This is a disorder –
> a fear or a thought
> Will NEVER do it!

I covered this card with sticky-backed plastic and to this day keep it in my handbag as a constant reminder for when my OCD rears its head. 'It's not me, it's my OCD' has now become a mantra for me whenever I feel troubled. Another card that I keep in my handbag has the following on it:

> Thoughts come because they
> frighten me and it's the
> fear that drives them
> (vicious circle)

On the reverse is the following:

1 Ian has shown that this is obsessional thinking – I will never do it.

2 I've had the thoughts lots of times and nothing has happened.

3 I can write down the events – and gain the evidence.

4 Taps – I have proved I can reduce the checking.

5 The thoughts are fantasised fears – NOT real actions.

6 It's an obsessional problem – different part of the brain from someone who does inflict harm.

I have used both of these cards to help me believe in myself. When you are feeling very anxious it isn't always easy to do so, but the cards can be a real help.

A combination of depression, OCD and various life events has resulted in me being seen by Ian over a number of years. I have been very lucky in having such a good mentor. The combination of working with him, medication and a determination not to be completely defeated by the OCD has meant that I have been able to enjoy life far more than previously. I now enjoy going to the cinema and being able to concentrate on the film! More importantly for me, I've been able to go to the theatre and see one of my favourite actors, Patrick Stewart, in *Macbeth* and *Waiting for Godot* without the productions being spoilt by continuous thoughts that I might have hurt somebody who is sitting directly in front of me!

I've always felt safe in my own home because of the circuit breakers. Over the years more and more homes have had them installed; knowing circuit breakers have been fitted enables me to visit other people's homes without feeling so tense, but I never enquire whether they have been fitted. In the past I have found it difficult to completely relax in other people's houses – even at my mother's home. So I was so greatly relieved when a few years ago she decided to have her house rewired. This didn't stop all of the thoughts but at least I could feel more comfortable when visiting or staying there. I am also able to visit my son without too much anxiety because his flat has circuit breakers installed. Over the last two or three years I've visited him several times and have usually been able to relax. Only once, during a stay there have I asked him to check an appliance. He needed some shirts ironed and I ironed them while he was at work. It was a steam iron and when it had cooled down I put it back into its box and then into the cupboard where he kept it. For some reason, perhaps it was the fact that I knew it wouldn't be used again whilst I was there, the iron began to prey on my mind. Perhaps I had put the plug in the sink? I did not want the rest of my time with him to be spoilt so, when he returned to the flat, I asked him to check it for me. I knew that if I took it out again and put it away this pattern could go on to be repeated several times and it seemed to me that the best way of dealing with this was to ask him to help me. When he had put the iron away again my anxiety slowly diminished and I began to relax more. Why this had to flare up that particular day I'm not sure because I have slept in his bedroom with a glass of water by my side and numerous electrical items in his room on many occasions. I've even painted watercolours with a jar of water beside his keyboard and three computers.

Nearly two years ago, I saw an advertisement for a cruise. I had mentioned to my son in the past that I would really love to go on one and so when I saw the advertisement I passed the paper to him. I certainly didn't expect him to say that he would go with me but once he had said that he would I was determined to do it. It was a trip to the Baltic Sea and it was one of the few cruise ships that does not allow children on it. This suited us both, particularly me as I would have no anxieties about worrying that I might pick up a child and throw it overboard. True, there would be electricity and water but I reasoned that there would be circuit breakers. In addition, by this stage I had told my son about my problems and I knew that if I were to have any difficulties he would reassure me. As luck would have it, my sixtieth birthday would occur during the holiday. So it really was to be a holiday of a lifetime.

Many years ago, if I had been given the opportunity to go on a cruise I would have been extremely hesitant. I would have found every excuse not to go if there had been children aboard. If it had been a childfree ship, I knew the cruise would still be marred by my thoughts. For example, I would have continually worried that I had left a tap running, immersed a hairdryer in a bowl full of water, poured a kettle full of water into the television, and so on. I would have relaxed slightly when I disembarked to visit a port. Now, however, I felt confident that I would be able to enjoy the holiday far, far more. After all, I had my cards to take with me and I also knew much more about the illness and had learnt techniques to help me with my anxiety. I was also determined that the bully was not going to win and spoil my holiday! Further, I was going with my son who would help me if I really needed him to do so. There was also one other thing I could do to help myself and that was to write a letter to myself.

This story has been about my OCD and I haven't really gone into much detail about my depression. However, one of the most useful skills that has helped me with my depression has also really helped me with my OCD, and that has been learning to recognize how my self-criticism undermines me and how to switch to a more compassionate, understanding, warm and encouraging way of thinking. Part of this has involved writing compassionate letters to myself. It is a technique that Ian has taught me. To begin with, the first few compassionate letters that I wrote were far from compassionate! Ian had to do a lot of correcting of them so that I learnt how to write to myself compassionately – as a friend would do. The aim was for me to try to imagine the friend speaking in soft soothing tones. People who have depression and OCD can be very hard on themselves and I certainly was. I really had to work hard at this part of my therapy. I would write a letter on the computer and then correct it. A few days later I would come back to it, read it through and improve on it again. I find having the collection of letters a useful reminder of how far I have come. The hard work has paid off as writing letters has been so therapeutic for me. So before I went on the cruise I wrote a long letter to myself, which I hoped would help me on the cruise. In this letter I reminded myself of how I had coped before and what strategies I could use if the OCD became a problem. The letter is written from the point of view of a close friend who knows how difficult I find it to go on holiday and who wishes me well. Here is part of the letter:

> *I know that you are somewhat concerned that the whole holiday might be spoilt by these fears. That is a very understandable fear considering your long history of obsessional thoughts! Just because these thoughts have occurred in the past does not mean that they will happen now. However if you start to get upset remember the 'kind voice' reminding you to accept the anxiety and telling you how sorry it is that you have to go through this . . .*

I took the letter with me and, as I expected, found that I did not need it until I was nearing the end of the cruise. I knew I could not come back to the ship to check whether I had done anything wrong but reading the letter to myself and referring to the OCD cards helped to remind me that while I'd had these thoughts many times before, I had never once acted upon them. I did not ask my son to check for me and when I got home I felt really proud of myself and so did Ian! I'd had my holiday of a lifetime and will have the memories forever. The bully had not won!

So where am I now? I have accepted my OCD as part of me but I still do hate this illness. Writing this story is another step on my journey towards being more open about having OCD. Slowly the shame I have felt over many, many years has been reduced. When I first went to see Ian I had hoped that my OCD would disappear completely and it was sometime later that Ian told me that because my OCD was so ingrained it may never totally disappear. I confess that I was disappointed but not surprised because I'd had OCD for at least twenty years without getting any help. He told me that I would need to learn to accept it and tolerate it far more. That is so. I now feel far more relaxed at home and at my son's flat. Last time I visited him I cooked for us both without hardly any rinsing of vegetables, etc. I can write letters and post them after one reading to check for spelling mistakes. I leave my home without checking that all is well – I now trust myself far more. I also go to an art class, which is held in a science laboratory! Unfortunately I still do find it difficult to go away on holiday. I cannot/will not ask a taxi driver to return to my home to check something again. I have built in various coping strategies to help me. For example, before I go away I always put the gas and the water off at the mains and switch off the circuit breakers to the shower and the hot water tank. Obviously some electricity has to be left on but wherever possible I pull plugs out of their sockets. If one of these plugs is causing me problems I try to put it in a position where I can remember where I last placed it. Last time I placed the plug to my electric blanket in the drawer of my bed! I feel all of this is worth it if it means that I can enjoy my holiday. I realize that these rituals are not ideal and they show that I have not managed to completely defeat the bully, but I do check far, far less than I used to.

Fortunately, in our society the stigma of having a mental illness is slowly being eroded. I never knew that I had a mental illness, but thanks to programmes such as the detective series *Monk* and articles in newspapers and magazines more and more people are aware of OCD. I am so glad that people are beginning to talk about this illness and admitting that they have it. We still have a way to go, as there are many people who don't want to admit to having any mental illness. Indeed, a member of my own family will not admit that they have OCD. I don't talk to them about it and so if they should read this book and recognize my story they would probably be quite surprised. OCD can very occasionally be hereditary but, thankfully, my son shows no sign of inheriting this illness. In the last few years several celebrities such as David Beckham have admitted to having OCD and this must help to remove some of the stigma of having a mental illness. If the stigma is removed sufferers of OCD may be more willing to get help and the sooner they do so the better for them it will be.

If you believe that you may have OCD and it is affecting your life please go and see your GP and get some help. If you do, it is more than likely that your OCD may be cured or certainly considerably improved. If you have a friend whom you suspect may have OCD probe gently and, again, if possible persuade them to get some help. While I am making progress and am able to do so much more than I used to, I realize that my treatment may well have progressed more quickly if I had received help sooner.

I am so very grateful to my GP for not giving up on me during those years when I saw him and refused to tell him what my problem was. Not every GP would have persevered like he did. I've also been extremely lucky in having Ian help me to come to terms with having OCD and learning to cope with it. He has enabled me to enjoy my life far more and I will always be very thankful to him for taking me on as his patient. Both my GP and Ian have made such a difference to my life. One of the things that I still find difficult is when I'm told that we all have thoughts like these as this makes me feel so incompetent for not being able to dismiss them. So if you do say this to someone please follow it up by saying something to the effect that you understand their problem and how difficult it must be for them. Show some compassion for them and their troubles.

Finally, as I write this, I am looking forward to a second cruise with my son. I shall take my original letter, my cards and the memory of how I coped last time with me. I hope to enjoy it as much as I did the last one, if not more!

Support groups, charities and other resources for obsessive compulsive disorder

Support groups and charities

United Kingdom

OCD Action
Suite 506–7 Davina House
137–49 Goswell Road
London EC1V 7ET, UK
Tel: 020 7253 2664
Helpline: 0845 390 6232
Email: support@ocdaction.org.uk
Website: www.ocdaction.org.uk

OCD UK
PO Box 8955
Nottingham NG10 9AU, UK
Email: admin@ocduk.org
Website: www.ocduk.org

United States of America

Obsessive Compulsive Foundation
676 State Street
New Haven, CT 06511, USA
Tel: 203 401 2070
Fax: 203 401 2076
Email: info@ocfoundation.org
Website: www.ocfoundation.org

Canada

Obsessive Compulsive Information and Support Centre, Inc.
204–825 Sherbrook Street
Winnipeg
Manitoba R3A 1M5, Canada
Tel: (204) 942 3331
Fax: (204) 975 3027
Email: occmanitoba@shaw.ca
Website: www.members.shaw.ca/occmanitoba/

Australia

Anxiety Recovery Centre Victoria
Obsessive Compulsive and Anxiety Disorders Foundation of Victoria (Inc)
42 High Street Road
Ashwood, VIC 3147, Australia
Tel: OCD and Anxiety Helpline 03 9886 9377
Office Line 03 9886 9233
Fax: 03 9886 9411
Email: arcmail@arcvic.com.au
Website: www.arcvic.com.au

Obsessive Compulsive Disorders Support Service Inc.
Room 318, Epworth Building
33 Pirie Street
Adelaide, SA 5000, Australia
Tel: 08 8231 1588
Fax: 08 8221 5159

New Zealand

OCD Support Group
Floor 2, Securities House
221 Gloucester Street
PO Box 13
167 Canterbury, New Zealand
Tel: (03) 366 6560
Fax: (03) 377 9665
Email: info@ocd.org.nz
Website: www.ocd.org.nz

Professional groups

Association for Advancement of Behavioral and Cognitive Therapies
305 7th Avenue
16th Floor
New York, NY 10001, USA
Tel: 212 647 1890
Fax: 212 647 1865
Website: www.aabt.org

The Australian Association for Cognitive and Behavior Therapy
Website: www.aacbt.org

British Association for Behavioural and Cognitive Psychotherapies (BABCP)
Imperial House, Hornby Street
Bury BL9 5BN
Tel: 0161 705 4304
Fax: 0161 705 4306
Email: babcp@babcp.com
Website: www.babcp.com

The European Association for Behavioural and Cognitive Therapists has a list of
member associations
Website: www.eabct.com

Websites and bulletin boards for OCD sufferers

www.angelfire.com/il/TeenOCD/
www.ocdaction.org.uk/ocdaction/index.asp?id=73
www.geonius.com/ocd/
http://groups.google.com/group/alt.support.ocd/topics?lnk=gschg
www.healthyplace.com/Communities/ocd/sandra/
http://understanding_ocd.tripod.com/index.html

Books

Overcoming Obsessive Compulsive Disorder by David Veale and Ros Wilson,
Robinson (2005).
Overcoming Obsessive Thoughts: How to Gain Control Over OCD by David Clark
and Christine Purdon, New Harbinger (2005).

Touch and Go Joe: An Adolescent's Experience of OCD by Joe Wells, Jessica Kingsley (2006).

The OCD Workbook: Your Guide to Breaking Free from Obsessive Compulsive Disorder by Bruce Hymen and Cherry Pedrick, New Harbinger (2010).

When Once is Not Enough by Gail S. Steketee and Kerrin White, New Harbinger (1991).

Get Out of My Head!: My Life with OCD by Allison Islin and Judy Karbritz, Poetry Press (2006).